T0407182

Studies in Public Choice

Series Editor

Randall G. Holcombe
Florida State University, Tallahassee, Florida, USA

Founding Editor

Gordon Tullock
George mason University, Fairfax, Virginia, USA

For other titles published in this series, go to
www.springer.com/series/6550

Keith L. Dougherty • Julian Edward

The Calculus of Consent and Constitutional Design

 Springer

Keith L. Dougherty
Department of Political Science
University of Georgia
Athens Georgia 30602
USA
dougherk@uga.edu

Julian Edward
Department of Mathematics
Florida International University
Miami Florida 33199
USA
edwardj@fiu.edu

ISSN 0924-4700
ISBN 978-0-387-98170-3   e-ISBN 978-0-387-98171-0
DOI 10.1007/978-0-387-98171-0
Springer New York Dordrecht Heidelberg London

Library of Congress Control Number: 2011923652

Printed on acid-free paper

Springer is part of Springer Science+Business Media (www.springer.com)

Praise for The Calculus of Consent and Constitutional Design

"The Calculus of Consent is one of the founding documents of the Public Choice school, and one of the most important books in political science in the last century. So it takes an ambitious book to promise to extend, and in some cases correct, the Buchanan and Tullock work. But Dougherty and Edward deliver on that promise. Make no mistake: this is much more than a reevaluation and update of the classic work. Dougherty and Edward bring these classic debates back to life, using the most recent literature and techniques. This book will be on dozens of graduate reading lists within a year of being published." - Michael Munger, Professor of Political Science and Professor of Economics, Duke University and Past President, Public Choice Society

"Dougherty and Edwards have written an excellent book. Its title echoes the classic work by Buchanan and Tullock. The authors re-examine, formalize and provide new insights into some of the main issues addressed in that classic and examine alternative properties of various electoral mechanisms. This book will be of significant interest to both political scientists and practitioners." - Annick Laruelle and Federico Valenciano, University of the Basque Country and Ikerbasque, authors of Voting and Collective Decision (2008)

To my wife Anjali and mother Bonnie, so they may know how much I love them.
   -Keith

To my wife Pam and children William, Deirdre, and Isaac, who with their love have kept me mostly sane.
   -Julian

Preface

By titling our book *The Calculus of Consent and Constitutional Design* we have undoubtedly attracted fans of Buchanan and Tullock's work, *The Calculus of Consent: Logical Foundations of Constitutional Democracy*, as well as those who might accuse us of coming from some conservative school before reading our work.

We are neither proponents nor opponents of Buchanan and Tullock's classic book. Instead, we are objective researchers interested in several of the same themes. We titled our book after theirs because their book inspired our research on related subjects. This includes questions such as, how do societies form constitutions in normatively appealing ways, and what is the best k-majority rule for legislative decision making when decision costs are large enough to be an important part of the decision? We also examine the properties of various electoral mechanisms that Buchanan and Tullock did not address in *The Calculus of Consent*.

In cases where some of their assumptions were vague, we have sometimes made assumptions that we found to be reasonable, rather than scouring their works to find the correct meaning. In other cases, we have adopted assumptions of our own. In this sense, we may be accurately accused of deviating from the original book. We can also be accused of deviating because we examine only some of their original themes. *The Calculus of Consent* covered a lot of ground. Formalizing and extending the arguments we missed is worthy of further investigation.

We hope that those who admire *The Calculus of Consent* will find our book to be a careful formalization and extension of some of the foundational parts of Buchanan and Tullock's earlier work. We often arrive at different conclusions, not because we did not like Buchanan and Tullock's original conclusions, but because they were the logical consequences of the models we examined or because we found evidence that drove us in a different direction. Anyone who is serious about a topic will want to expand its teachings and carefully investigate its mechanisms rather than simply reiterate the conclusion that was originally written.

For those who somehow view *The Calculus of Consent* with a tainted eye, we hope they find our book devoid of such taint. In addition to extending a book that had a big impact on political science and to a lesser extent economics, we raise questions about how constitutions are formed and how they ought be formed in a way that should be useful to any student of constitutional design. Perhaps others will follow our footsteps and try to formalize other classic works.

We are indebted to several people. In particular, Jac Heckelman helped us select voting rules and criteria for our chapter on elections and to find some key studies in that literature. Jie Mi helped clarify some concepts pertaining to conditional probabilities used in our probabilistic arguments. The data on delegate votes from the U.S. Constitutional Convention were gathered with the support of the National Science Foundation, Grant No. SES-0752098, Keith Dougherty and Jac Heckelman investigators. Any opinions, findings, and conclusions or recommendations expressed in this material are those of the author(s) and do not necessarily reflect the views of the National Science Foundation or the others we have acknowledged.

Keith L. Dougherty   *Athens, Georgia*
Julian Edward   *Miami, Florida*
January, 2011

Contents

Chapter 1
Introduction

A wave of economic and political liberalization is sweeping the world. Many countries in Latin America and Eastern Europe have made transitions from semi-closed to open societies and from authoritarian governments to liberal democracies. In several of these cases, the transition has been accompanied by a new constitution that purports to increase the fairness and efficiency of the regime. Some who adopt these new constitutions are interested in manipulating policies for their narrow interests. Others are interested in writing constitutions that reflect the concerns of the populace and provide greater legitimacy for their government.

From a purely American perspective, studying the properties of a good constitutional design may seem more like an arcane examination of an outdated historical event than a serious study of contemporary politics. The U.S. Constitution is over 200 years old and it has been rarely amended. Yet the U.S. Constitution is the exception, not the rule. Between 1787 and 2008, the average U.S. state has lived under three different constitutions, and its constitution(s) have been amended more than 144 times. Louisiana has been governed by eleven constitutions and its constitutions have been amended 154 times (Council of State Governments, 2009). Internationally, "we have moved from a situation where almost no country had a written constitution to one where almost every country has one" (Lutz, 2006). The international transformation is partly due to the break up of the Soviet Union and the birth of new democracies Latin America and Eastern Europe. But it is also due to a widespread desire to improve governmental institutions. In fact, between 1974 and 1988 more than half of the countries in the world entirely rewrote their constitution (Voigt, 1997).

With the desire to continually create new constitutions, the natural question is how should a society write such a beast? What institutions will legitimize the state and promote desirable outcomes? By "institutions" we mean the rules and processes that control government functions. These include, but are not limited to, unicameralism versus bicameralism, the extent to which executive and legislative functions are separate, and the powers of the judiciary. They also include more fundamental questions about the voting rules used in various phases of government. Majority rule is only one example.

There are at least three contexts that need voting rules. First, voting rules are usually adopted to make decisions about the constitution itself. In other words, to make decision about how to decide. Second, voting rules are used by legislative bodies to make day-to-day decisions on policy. Third, voting rules are used to elect politicians.

This book investigates these three phases of constitutional decision making critically and analytically. It follows the seminal work of Buchanan and Tullock's *The Calculus of Consent* in trying to unravel how contractarian arguments in political philosophy can help us implement constitutions.

When it was first released in 1962, *The Calculus of Consent* was considered a breakthrough in political science. At the time, theories of politics focused largely on the history of ideas (Friedrich, 1963). Riker (1962, p. 408) wrote, "political theory as a field of academic concentration has been in a confused and unproductive state for at least the last generation." Buchanan and Tullock's application of economic methods to subjects that were traditionally in the realm of political science helped break the deadlock and allowed political scientists to create their own models of politics. Riker argued that *The Calculus of Consent* was one of a few works that re-oriented political theory and helped to make political science more productive (Riker, 1962, p. 409).

Since then, *The Calculus of Consent* has been translated into five languages and is widely cited to this day by scholars studying preference revelation mechanisms, voting rules, legislative procedure, and public choice. Among the major contributions of the book is a connection between constitutional decision making and social contract theory — a philosophical tradition that aims to give institutions legitimacy.

Social contract theorists, such as Hobbes ([1651] 1962), Locke ([1690] 1988), and Rousseau ([1762] 1997) used the notion of unanimous consent to justify government and to codify moral norms. Although these scholars arrived at very different conclusions among themselves, they all emphasized that legitimate state authority must be derived from the consent of the governed. Each used a hypothetical state of nature to examine human behavior in the absence of government. In this state, the only constraints on individual actions are conscience decisions and human interactions. Social contract theorists use this vantage to attempt to explain, in different ways, why it is in an individual's interest to voluntarily surrender part or all of their sovereignty to a government that maintains social order. For example, Hobbes ([1651] 1962) describes a state of nature where individuals fight in a war of all against all. From this state, it is in an individual's interest to surrender his or her rights to all things, most notably the right to self-protection. Locke ([1690] 1988) describes a state of nature where property rights pre-exist. Individuals surrender less of their liberty in his argument because some major issues have already been resolved. Beyond the protection of property, government has a more limited role.

Buchanan and Tullock add to this tradition by moving away from the hypothetical development of a social contract to the actual adoption of constitutions. They ask which voting rules would rational people chose to adopt if property rights were already settled. They conclude that in the ideal case the optimal voting rule would be unanimity rule because it is the only voting rule that guarantees economic efficiency in the sense of Pareto superiority and Pareto optimality (an outcome where it is not possible to make anyone better off without making someone else worse off). If someone was made worse off by the constitution, gainers would be forced to compensated by the losers under unanimity rule. They would not be forced to make such compensations under majority rule.

This argument is particularly germane to the types of decisions made at the constitutional stage because society has no way to agree on how to agree at this stage. Hence, requiring everyone to agree seems natural. For the legislative stage of decision making the cumulative time and effort required to make decisions may suggest that other voting rules, such as majority rule, should be preferred. Buchanan and Tullock do not treat elections as a distinct category, as we do here. Instead, they briefly mention how the voting rules used by legislatures can be used in elections. Buchanan echoed these themes throughout his subsequent works and won the 1986 Nobel Prize in Economics partly for this research.

Even though *The Calculus of Consent* may be accurately classified as an extension of modern social contract theory, the book had a greater impact on other fields. As Rowley (2004, v.2, p. ix) writes, *The Calculus of Consent* "played a significant role in carving out two new disciplines from economics and political science — *public choice* (the analysis of politics as it is) and *constitutional political economy* (the analysis of politics as it should be)." Public choice applies economic methods to problems that are normally dealt with by political scientists, such as questions about voting, interest group formation, and rent seeking. Constitutional political economy investigates the creation of constitutions as well as the implications of some institutions that might be adopted. Our work makes a greater contribution to the latter tradition.

Although Buchanan and Tullock's work is used as a guidepost for our own study (also see Hardin 1988, 1999), we do not advocate nor disavow their position. We merely attempt to analyze three phases of constitutional decision making and to formalize some of their earlier claims. Since their claims were largely descriptive, as were most books written fifty years ago, we occasionally stray from their original ideas. These departures are not the result of insincerity. As is the case with any descriptive work, their assumptions are sometimes unclear, which forces us to fill in the gaps as best as we can. At other times their assumptions are clear, but we stray from their ideas because we think we have a better starting point and want to see the implications of slightly different assumptions.

When modeling the functioning of an assembly, there are two different elements that should be considered: (i) the human interplay that is expressed in the choice of proposal, bargaining, the decision to attend, etc., and (ii) the mathematical properties of the winning coalition. In this work, we emphasize the mathematical properties of the winning coalition, and do not assume bargaining or vote trading in our models. Both play important roles in *The Calculus of Consent*. However, we do not assume bargaining explicitly because we do not want to incorporate any black box processes into our theories. Instead, we allow for bargaining through the process of proposing and voting itself. Such processes are more applicable to large societies attempting to reach agreements than sit-down meetings where individuals are assumed to talk toward a mutually advantageous solution.

Our models for constitutional decision making allow for bargaining through the process of proposing, voting, and re-proposing to satisfy voters. Our models for legislative decision making presume that individuals are more likely to propose successful proposals as the number of rounds increases. Both could be driven by bargaining, but bargaining is not a necessary condition for either phenomena. In this way, we believe our models are more general and perhaps more realistic for questions of constitutional design. Readers are encouraged to read both *The Calculus of Consent* and our work to see how closely the two books are related to each other.[1]

We begin by summarizing the arguments developed by Buchanan and Tullock and how they relate to social contract theory. We then carefully define several concepts and relate them to Pareto optimality and Pareto improvements, two concepts widely used in the study of economic efficiency. This provides a backdrop for analyzing the three phases of constitutional decision making: (1) the constitutional phase, where rules for constitutional decision making must be justified; (2) the legislative phase, which governs day-to-day decision making; and (3) the electoral phase, where the optimal voting rule for large electorates and potentially more than two alternatives are determined. These phases differ by context and sources of legitimacy.

1.1 Three Stages of Decision Making

Buchanan and Tullock divide democratic decision making into two stages: constitutional decision making and legislative decision making. We add a third stage — elections — because they are central to democracy and differ from the other two in kind.

Buchanan and Tullock view constitutional decisions as social contracts that bind all individuals. The most fundamental choice in a social contract is to determine which voting rules, and other institutions, will be used to make decisions in later phases of government. The decision is akin to deciding how to decide itself. According to Buchanan and Tullock, the most basic principle for such a decision is unanimity rule. Unanimity rule has a eminent place in constitutional decision making because it assures that rational individuals will come to mutually advantageous agreements as they would in an economic contract. Individuals will consent to a social contract only if they agree to its terms. Buchanan and Tullock argue in favor of unanimity rule because it requires all individuals to favor collectivization before society is allowed to collectivize. Individual are allowed to reject collectivization if

---

[1] We do not include vote trading simply because much of the foundational work, without vote trading, needed further development. Nevertheless, our work can be useful for those who want to study vote trading in future works. For instance, the mathematics on the difficulty of achieving a coalition of a given size can shed light on the depth of concessions needed to pass a piece of legislation with vote trading. We encourage scholars to work on such extensions.

it makes them worse off. Less-inclusive voting rules, such as majority rule, allow some individuals to create constitutions that coerce others against their will.

Legislative decisions are quite different. Because there can be incredible inefficiencies associated with the time and effort needed to negotiate unanimously agreed upon policies, individuals can agree at the constitutional stage to require a less-inclusive voting rule at the legislative stage. In this way, it is completely consistent for a society to require unanimity for constitutional decisions while requiring less-inclusive rules, such as majority rule, for legislative decisions. Because there are hundreds of policy decisions and only a few constitutional decisions, Buchanan and Tullock argue that rational individuals might recognize the expediency of making daily decisions using a less-inclusive voting rule, such as majority rule. Citizens cannot be forced to accept the use of such rules without their consent.

Electoral decisions, which were only briefly mentioned in the *Calculus of Consent*, are typically decisions about electing public officials. Because the electorate is usually quite large, vote trading among citizens is quite difficult.[2] Furthermore, elections can be unique because there is no status quo alternative unless an incumbent runs for re-election. In these cases, constitutional designers typically want to treat all candidates equally rather than favor a status quo candidate. This observation alone moves them away from the type of voting rules advocated for legislatures because the status quo plays an important role in those types of rules. Finally, since the costs of organizing a vote are usually high, citizens are unlikely to want to vote on a pair of alternatives, wait for the outcome, then return to the polls to vote on other pairs, several times. Sequencing votes through such an agenda is extremely rare in elections. Instead, elections are typically conducted with all the alternatives (candidates) considered at once. Any voting rule that wants to consider alternatives pairwise would typically have to gather that information in one or two votes. In legislatures, repetitive voting on different versions of the same bill is more widely accepted because legislatures are professionals expected to iron out the nuances of legislation. These three considerations imply that a different set of voting rules may be more appropriate for the electoral phase than those Buchanan and Tullock had in mind for the constitutional and legislative phases.

Central to the method of the current book are easy-to-understand computer-based simulations and powerful analytical tools used for studying the relationships between voting rules and democratic outcomes. This makes the book appealing to scholars in comparative politics who are interested in the role of institutions in the transition to democracy, democratic theorists interested in putting political philosophy into practice, and computer scientists and constitutional political economists attempting to see the application of a computer model to social science for the first time. It also provides a careful reconsideration of a classic work.

We start, in Chapter 2, by reviewing the arguments made by Buchanan and Tullock in their classic work *The Calculus of Consent*. Buchanan and Tullock (1962) and Mueller (1996, 2001) argued that government decision making should be divided into two phases: a constitutional phase and a parliamentary phase. These

---

[2] Nevertheless, Buchanan and Tullock (1962) make an interesting argument about different candidates representing implicit bundles of vote trades. See their pages 135–36.

phases correspond to the constitutional and legislative phases described in our book. A cornerstone of the earlier arguments is that the institutions passed at the constitutional phase should make some individuals better off without making other individuals worse off. Decisions made at the parliamentary phase have to balance such concerns with the desire to reduce the time and effort needed to make multiple decisions quickly.

In Chapter 3, we carefully define several concepts employed by Buchanan and Tullock and show why the relationships between unanimity rule and various Pareto principles may not be as closely linked as Buchanan and Tullock seem to suggest. This provides a backdrop for analyzing the three phases of decision making and illustrates how minor differences in definitions can lead to major differences in applications — particularly for medium- and large-sized populations. This has important implications for the use of Pareto concepts, particularly at the electoral phase of decision making. It also sets the stage for showing that other voting rules may be more capable of attaining Pareto optimal results than unanimity rule.

Chapter 4 examines voting in the constitutional phase where decision making costs are allegedly inconsequential. We use computer simulations and deductive techniques to analyze the claim that unanimity rule is better at producing Pareto superior and Pareto optimal results than other voting rules. We do this for settings where proposals are (1) random, (2) sincere, or (3) strategic. We find three interesting results, all related to Pareto optimality.

First, if individuals propose randomly, then majority rule is almost always more likely to select a Pareto optimal outcome than unanimity rule. Second, if individuals propose sincerely, then majority rule is at least as likely to select a Pareto optimal outcome as unanimity rule. Third, if individuals propose and vote strategically, then unanimity rule will always yield a Pareto optimal outcome. Other k-majority rules often yield a Pareto optimal outcome, and will always yield an outcome that is very nearly Pareto optimal. A k-majority rule is a majority rule, supermajority rule, or unanimity rule that requires a certain threshold of affirmative votes for a proposal to pass.[3]

In contrast, with rare exceptions for random proposals, unanimity rule is at least as likely as majority rule to select outcomes that are both Pareto superior and Pareto optimal. These findings suggest that unanimity rule is more capable of creating Pareto efficient constitutions only if efficiency requires everyone to be at least as well off as they are under the status quo. We support these findings with laboratory experiments and illustrate them with data from the adoption of the U.S. Constitution.

Chapter 5 examines voting in a legislative setting. In particular, we analyze the optimal k-majority rule in terms of both decision costs and external costs (defined later). In legislative settings, Buchanan and Tullock (1962) and Mueller (1996) claim that a k-majority rule near half the voting body would be preferred because this rule minimizes the sum of these two costs.

We examine external costs and decision costs over a sequence of votes. The introduction of multiple alternatives affects external costs and decision making costs

---

[3] For example, the U.S. House of Representatives requires 218 of its 435 members to sign a successful discharge petition. In this case, $k = 218$. More precise definitions are offered in Chapter 3.

in two ways. First, multiple alternatives forces us to re-examine the shape of the external cost function and to compare it to the two alternative case (Dougherty and Edward, 2004, p. 171). Second, with multiple alternatives, our analysis of decision making costs becomes more sophisticated and allows us to make conjectures about the conditions under which specific k-majority rules minimize total costs. We find that the optimal k-majority is largely determined by the weight that decision makers put on these two functions, the latent propensity to pass proposals, and the quickness with which favorable proposals can be found. Majority rule is only optimal under stylized conditions unless there is a jump discontinuity in the decision cost function as conjectured by Mueller (2003).

In Chapter 6, we compare the properties of four voting rules, three of which are widely used in elections. Because electoral decisions require voting among an extremely large number of individuals and there is no reason to adopt voting rules that favor the status quo, k-majority rules are rarely, if ever, employed. Instead, plurality rule, majority rule with a runoff, and instant runoff voting are examined because they are widely used to elect officials in single-member districts. We also include the Borda count because it has received recent attention in the social choice literature. With so many voters almost all candidates are Pareto optimal and the Pareto criterion is of little use in analyzing mass elections. Instead, we evaluate these rules using six normative criteria separately: (i) the Condorcet winner criterion, (ii) the Condorcet loser criterion, (iii) the majority criterion, (iv) consistency, (v) reversal symmetry, and (vi) independence of eliminated alternatives. We conduct our analysis using computer simulations of single-dimensional voting in single-member districts. This allows us to determine the probability that each voting rule adheres to a criterion in a context that is widely assumed in the literature. We find the Borda count outperforms the other three voting rules in terms of the independence of eliminated alternatives, and it performs at least as well as the other voting rules on the Condorcet loser criterion, consistency, and reversal symmetry. Majority rule with a runoff always adheres to the majority criterion (while Borda count does not) and it avoids Condorcet losers. It also performs almost perfectly in terms of consistency and reversal symmetry. Which of the two voting rules perform better on the Condorcet winner criterion depends on the conditions. Hence, the best voting rule may depend on what each society values most.

The book concludes with a few comments about the significance of our research for social contract theory and the creation of constitutions more broadly.

By examining impartial standards and showing which sets of institutions are most likely to fulfill these standards, academics can recommend fairer institutions in a wide variety of settings. Such results help us recommend the most desirable voting rules for countries writing new constitutions (such as Afghanistan and Iraq), for policy makers creating institutions for local municipalities, and for legislatures reconsidering their own voting rules (such as the U.S. Senate reconsidering the filibuster). They can also help us guide smaller voting bodies such as a board of directors or a university senate that wants to establish its own, fairer, and more efficient rules for decision making.

Chapter 2
Original Theories and Current Studies

When the first author was a graduate student, some of his professors would argue about the five most influential works in formal political theory. Their lists included classics that affected a wide audience, not just works that were technically advanced. Kenneth Arrow's *Social Choice and Individual Values*, Mancur Olson's *Logic of Collective Action*, and Anthony Downs' *An Economic Theory of Democracy* frequently made the list. Others were discussed, but Buchanan and Tullock's *The Calculus of Consent* always seemed to be in the top five.

When it was first published, *The Calculus of Consent* contained a number of fresh ideas. Buchanan and Tullock argued that no voting rule is flawless because there is always a tradeoff between decision costs and external costs. Decision costs are the time and effort needed to make a decision. External costs are the losses an individual expects to endure as the result of the coercive actions of others. Majority rule imposes moderate amounts of decision costs and external costs. Unanimity rule imposes no external costs but considerable decision costs. Whether one of these voting rules, or perhaps a supermajority rule, should be adopted depends on the context.

This chapter reviews the arguments made by Buchanan and Tullock in their classic work, *The Calculus of Consent*. We first detail Buchanan and Tullock's argument for determining the optimal k-majority rule in a legislature. We examine legislative decision making first, before constitutional decision making, because it facilitates our descriptions of constitutional decision making in the next section. The constitutional stage contains potentially high external costs relative to decision costs, making it arguable different from legislative decision making. In this setting, unanimity rule is considered an ideal type. In the next section, we briefly describe Buchanan and Tullock's thoughts on some additional themes, such as vote trading and representative democracy. We then end the chapter with a very brief discussion of how their book influenced later works.

2.1 Legislative Decision Making

Central to Buchanan and Tullock's study of legislative decision making is the examination of various k-majority rules. Loosely, under k-majority rule a proposal needs k "yea" votes to pass; otherwise the proposal is rejected. These can range from the affirmative vote of one individual to the affirmative vote of all N individuals in the population. Buchanan and Tullock analyze the optimal k-majority rule using two types of costs: external costs and decision making costs. The optimal k-majority rule is the one that minimizes the sum of these two costs.

External costs are the expected costs an individual endures as the result of the actions of others (Buchanan and Tullock, 1962, p. 64). Buchanan and Tullock argue that these costs are a decreasing function of the number of individuals required to agree to group decisions. This is because members of the decisive coalition will consider their own marginal costs and can easily make decisions contrary to the interests of people outside their coalition. At one extreme, external costs will be greatest if a single individual can authorize action for the group. On the other extreme, external costs will be lowest, typically zero, if everyone in the group is required to agree. The latter occurs because individuals will not allow others to impose external costs on them if each has the power to reject decisions that can hurt them (Buchanan and Tullock, 1962, p. 64).[1]

To illustrate the idea, Buchanan and Tullock (1962, pp. 66–7) consider a municipality issuing property taxes to pay for street repairs. If one individual is allowed to decide which streets are repaired, and that individual maximizes his/her personal net benefits, he/she would spend the money on the roads on which he/she travels and neglect the roads used by others. Of course, the individual who is dictating road repairs would not experience external costs. However, the individuals governed by the decision who are not in the decisive coalition would be likely to incur positive external costs. At the other extreme, if everyone in the municipality had to give their approval for street repairs, each individual would approve of the road repair only if it gave them positive net benefits. Without knowing whether an individual will be a member of the decisive coalition, an individual can expect large external costs if one individual is allowed to dictate repairs and zero external costs if all individuals must agree on repairs.

In describing external costs, Buchanan and Tullock clearly have the *expected* incurred by an individual in mind. Presumably no one knows *a priori* whether they will be a member of the decisive coalition or someone outside the decisive coalition. Instead, they have to make a decision about the most appropriate k-majority rule as if they could be in either position. For this reason, expected external costs should decrease as the number of individuals required to make a decision increases. Actual external costs may or may not decrease for each individual.

In contrast, decision making costs are the costs resulting from the time and effort needed to reach an agreement. Buchanan and Tullock argue that such costs are an

---

[1] See Heckelman and Dougherty (2010a) for a crude test of whether larger k-majority rules have negative effects on various tax increases.

increasing function of the number of individuals needed to make a decision. Very little time and effort is needed for one individual to make a decision because that person does not have to negotiate an agreement with anyone else. More time is required as the number required to assent increases, partly because members of the decisive coalition will have fewer members outside their coalition to turn to if someone in their coalition opposes their proposal.

In the street repair example, requiring the approval of only one individual to make decisions may lead to quick decisions about street repairs. Requiring a few more individuals in the decisive coalition will require a little more time and effort to craft plans. If everyone must approve, a considerable amount of time and effort is required to make sure that everyone is satisfied with the plan and to thwart any jockeying for larger shares.

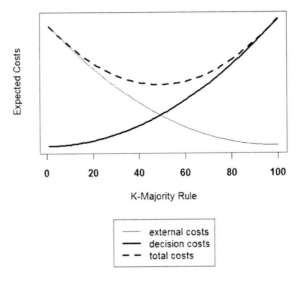

Fig. 2.1 Traditional External Costs and Decision Costs

Buchanan and Tullock (1962, pp. 65-71) represent such costs in a figure similar to the one depicted in Figure 2.1. The expected costs of a particular decision are represented along the vertical axis and the number of individuals required to make a decision are represented along the horizontal axis. The thin line, which decreases from left to right, depicts external costs. The thick line, which increases from left to right, depicts decision costs. At the left extreme, the rule of anyone making decisions for the group produces potentially large external costs but minimal decision costs. No delays should be expected under that voting rule. On the right extreme, unanimity rule minimizes external costs but imposes extremely high decision making costs. Buchanan and Tullock suggest that the optimal decision making rule minimizes the sum of these two functions (depicted by the dashed line). This occurs at $k = 49$

in this particular figure. Here the sum of the expected costs from having a decision imposed on oneself and the expected costs of making decisions is minimized. If legislatures have to chose a voting rule from the set of k-majority rules, $k = 49$ would be optimal.

In making such claims, Buchanan and Tullock do not prescribe an ideal set of institutions for every society. Instead, they recommend that each country, town, or local club adopt their own set of institutions based on how individuals within their society value these two costs. In this sense *The Calculus of Consent* (1962) creates an interplay between positive observations about how rational individuals choose and normative recommendations about how they ought to choose. On the one hand, rational individuals make choices about which institutions to adopt. These choices are positive. On the other hand, Buchanan and Tullock's recommendations about how constitutional decisions ought to be made is very normative. Because different societies, and different individuals within societies, value different properties, it is logically consistent for different societies to chose different sets of institutions and for all of them to be fair. Furthermore, a society may find decision costs negligible for the constitutional phase and use unanimity rule to make a decision about the optimal k-majority for legislation, then adopt some less inclusive k-majority rule, such as majority rule, for the legislative decisions. As Buchanan and Tullock write, "there is no necessary inconsistency implied in the adoption of, say, simple majority rule for the making of certain everyday decisions for the group with respect to those activities that have been explicitly collectivized, and the insistence on unanimity of consensus on changes in the fundamental organizational rules" (Buchanan and Tullock, 1962, p. 251).

However, some properties may guide individuals in their choice of the optimal k-majority rule. Everything else equal, decision costs should be greater when there are a variety of opinions and information is scarce than when opinions are homogenous and the information is readily available. Similarly, larger communities may have greater difficulty making decisions than smaller ones, which means they have larger decision costs. Furthermore, communities that have well-written bills of rights might expect lower external costs than communities without such protections (Mueller, 2003, p. 76).

Buchanan and Tullock's analysis suggests that if both external costs and decision costs are relevant to the decision, then the optimal k-majority rule will be between 1 and N. Majority rule is just one of the many candidates. There is no *a priori* reason why majority rule would be the k-majority rule that minimizes total costs.

Others have adjusted Buchanan and Tullock's argument in a way that makes majority rule much more likely to be optimal. For example, Mueller (2003, pp. 76-8) claims that there might be a "kink" in the decision cost function at $N/2$.[2] The reason is that for any $k \leq n/2$, it is possible for both policy A and policy $\sim A$ to pass. For example suppose k is set to 35 out of 100 voters. A proposal to increase school expenditures might first receive a winning majority of say 40 voters. After the measure passes, a counterproposal to cut school expenditures by the same margin

---

[2] By "kink" Mueller meant a jump discontinuity.

could also pass. This is because any k-majority rule with $k \leq 50$ allows a winning coalition to be found on both sides of the issue. An assembly that adopts such a rule can be deadlocked in an endless series of offsetting proposals. Such proposals would increase decision making costs dramatically. Since the argument applies to any $k \leq 50$, but not for $k > 50$, decision costs will jump upwards at $k = 50$, as depicted in Figure 2.2. The function remains continuous elsewhere. Such a jump discontinuity typically places the minimum at majority rule. Although the exact k-majority that minimizes total costs still depends on the shape of the decision cost curve and the relative value of external costs and decision costs by individual members, Mueller's argument provides an explanation for why majority rule is so common in practice (Mueller, 2003, pp. 76–8).

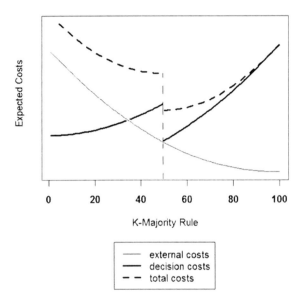

Fig. 2.2 Mueller's Big Jump Discontinuity

Others have expanded on Buchanan and Tullock's original ideas. In a separate work, Mueller (2003, p. 103) argues that vote cycling might make decision costs U-shaped with a minimum around 64% of the population.[3] Combined with the previous argument against k-majority rules less than majority rule, this might make the optimal k-majority around 64% of the voters. Spindler (1990) argues that legislative decisions should also include rent-seeking costs. With rent-seeking costs included, total costs might be minimized closer to unanimity rule or to the rule of one than to majority rule. Guttman (1998) claims that the optimal k-majority rule should be

---

[3] Caplin and Nalebuff (1988) show that 64% is the minimum size of the k-majority coalition that guarantees no vote cycling.

based on the Kaldor–Hicks criterion and concludes that majority rule is most suitable for that standard. Rae (1969) in contrast, defines the optimal k-majority rule as the one that minimizes the probability of society choosing against an individual. Analyzing two alternative cases in a probabilistic setting, Rae concludes that majority rule is most capable of making such choices.[4] Finally, Brennan and Hamlin (2000) replace the external cost function with an agency loss function and apply a similar analysis to the optimal proportion of representatives in a representative democracy. In all of these cases, except perhaps the work of Rae, external costs and decision costs are not fully formalized. Instead, the argument is written as an analytical narrative. One of goal of this book is to develop more careful formalizations of these concepts.

2.2 Constitutional Decision Making

For Buchanan and Tullock constitutional decisions are quite different from legislative decisions because constitutional decisions establish the rules of the game and dictate the legislative process well into the future. In constitutional settings, individuals are less certain about their future circumstances and interests. This uncertainty makes them think more objectively and behave as if they were the average person in a constitutional setting (Buchanan and Tullock, 1962, pp. 77–80).

The argument is somewhat reminiscent of Kant's categorical imperative, which suggests that individuals ought to make choices that apply to all similarly situated individuals. This does not suggest that individuals will always agree about which institutions are best. It only explains why Buchanan and Tullock believe constitutional decisions are more impartial than policy decisions. This impartiality causes decision makers to become more homogenous, which in turn reduces decision costs.

Moreover, when rational individuals consider the importance of constitutional decisions and note that one constitutional decision can govern thousands of policy decisions, they may be willing to ignore decision costs and evaluate constitutional decisions solely on the basis of external costs. Buchanan and Tullock believe that without decision costs, unanimity rule is clearly the best voting rule. They write, "this single decision-making rule acquires a unique position in our whole analysis which suggests that if costs of decision-making could be reduced to negligible proportions, the rational individual should always support the requirement of unanimous consent" (1962, p. 88).

Buchanan and Tullock recognize that decision making costs are likely to be positive at the constitutional stage of decision making (pp. 94–5). They simply argue that making decisions about the rules of the game implies potentially large external costs — so large that the relative importance of decision costs is negligible.

---

[4] Rae assumes voters are equally likely to support or oppose a proposal and that everyone votes. If different assumptions are made, then his model does not necessarily predict that majority rule is optimal.

Requiring any threshold less than unanimity would leave the rational individual uncertain about whether they would be a member of the decisive coalition or the non-decisive coalition. It would make it possible for them to be made worse off by the creation of a collective with coercive powers. In contrast, unanimity rule includes everyone in the bargain and guarantees Pareto improvements. That is, it guarantees change that make at least one person better off and no one else worse off. A point where no additional improvements like this can be made is considered Pareto optimal.[5]

Pareto optimality is the most widely accepted measure of efficiency in welfare economics. By connecting consensual decision making to unanimity rule and unanimity rule to the concept of a Pareto improvement, Buchanan and Tullock are able to connect classic political philosophy to modern conceptions of efficiency. Buchanan and Tullock write, "[t]he welfare-political-economist approach indicates that a specific choice is Pareto optimal only if all parties reach agreement. ... [A]ll less-than-unanimity decision-making rules can be expected to lead to nonoptimal decisions by the Pareto criterion" (1962, pp. 94–95).[6] In this sense unanimity rule becomes the "ideal" voting rule and deviations from unanimity rule are seen as necessary expedients (p. 96).

Some of the most important constitutional decisions are whether the legislature will be unicameral or bicameral (Buchanan and Tullock, 1962, pp. 233–48), the proportion of the population that will act as representatives (Buchanan and Tullock, 1962, pp. 205-8), and the method of election — either as a function of individual votes or some randomization device (Buchanan and Tullock, 1962, pp. 217–20). It also includes the choice of the k-majority rule used in the legislature. That choice is a re-occurring theme throughout *The Calculus of Consent*.

Because each legislative decision will create its own decision costs, individuals will choose the best k-majority rule for the legislative phase by considering both external costs and decision making costs at the constitutional phase.

As various institutions are proposed and discussed at the constitutional phase, individuals make decisions about whether they want to opt into the collectivization or opt out. In addition to arguing that requiring k-majority rules less than unanimity allow some individuals to coerce others, Buchanan and Tullock argue that k-majority rules with $k < N$ may cause too many resources to be allocated to the public sector. This does not mean that the collectivization will be over-extended into unnatural issue areas, though the collective could overextend; it means that too many resources will be applied to the activities that the community collectivizes (Buchanan and Tullock, 1962, p. 205).

Buchanan and Tullock argue that orthodox arguments against unanimity rule as infeasible are based on choices between two mutually exclusive alternatives — such as a single status quo and a single proposal. They envision constitutional decision making that allows for bargaining over a whole array of alternatives (Buchanan and Tullock, 1962, pp. 253–4). To illustrate the point, they consider an example with

---

[5] Such concepts are defined more carefully in the next chapter.

[6] Also see Buchanan and Tullock (1962, pp. 94, 110)

three people deciding whether to collectivize fishing (Buchanan and Tullock, 1962, pp. 254–5). If the choice is to collectivize or not, one individual could be easily opposed to collectivizing fishing, perhaps because he does not like fish – in which case unanimity is very unlikely. However, if the decision also includes collectivizing the gathering of coconuts, then the three individuals may be able to logroll and find a collective agreement that make all three of them better off.

Of course, this logic extends to other activities as well. If they cannot find any agreement across all the possible activities that can be collectivized, collectiviz-ing would not be in everyone's mutual interest and imposing a coercive collective agreement on all three would be wrong. "When trades can take place, the analogy with economic or market exchange is appropriate" (Buchanan and Tullock, 1962, p. 255). Vote trading and bargaining help social contracts become more like economic contracts.

2.3 Representative Democracy

Buchanan and Tullock illustrate just how broad this idea can be applied when they examine representative democracy in Chapter 15. This chapter is the closest their work comes to analyzing elections as a separate phase of decision making. In it, they identify four basic constitutional choice variables that individuals must judge simul-taneously: (1) the voting rule used for choosing representatives (i.e., a k-majority rule applied to elections in various districts), (2) the basis of representation in the assembly (i.e., the proper mix of functional and random elements), (3) the degree of representation (i.e., the fraction of the population that will act as representatives), and (4) the k-majority rule used in an assembly to make decisions. Having already discussed the costs associated with the fourth variable, Buchanan and Tullock apply the same analysis to the other variables.

Consider the third variable. At one extreme, only one representative makes deci-sions on behalf of the voters. At the other extreme (direct democracy), the number of representatives equal the number of eligible voters. When constitutions enumer-ate the minimum number of representatives allowed in a population, they codify a choice about the degree of representation. That is, the proportion of the population that will be elected as representatives. Buchanan and Tullock argue that choosing the optimal number of representatives is similar to choosing the optimal k-majority rule — except in this case, the independent variable is the ratio of number of rep-resentative to the number of individuals in the population. Decision costs increase with larger proportions because the time it takes to make decisions increases as a greater proportion of individuals act as representatives. At the same time external costs should decrease as the proportion of the population acting as representatives increases.

The second variable, the basis of representation, determines the composition of representatives. At the one extreme, representatives will be elected as a function of individual votes. At the other extreme, all representatives may be drawn by say random lots as in ancient Athens. In the latter cases, political officials may still be considered representative, though in a different sense. Most democracies chose to keep random elements at a minimum, but that does not mean that the second variable is not a constitutional choice (Buchanan and Tullock, 1962, p. 218–9).

Buchanan and Tullock bring these four constitutional elements together and argue that at the constitutional stage, individuals attempt to minimize the sum of the combined costs in equilibrium. If others successfully propose to increase the k-majority rule used in elections, then decision costs will increase, external costs will decrease, and citizens may want to decrease the k-majority thresholds in variables two through four. If others propose a shift from a functional basis of representation to a more random one, expected decision costs will probably increase and expected external costs decrease. Individuals may then want to decrease the thresholds in variables one, three, and four to compensate (Buchanan and Tullock, 1962, p. 227–9). This suggests that the simple analytical model used to analyze voting thresholds in an assembly may be more general. It also demonstrates the complexity of decision making that Buchanan and Tullock hope individuals can handle.

2.4 Vote Trading and Other Themes

The proceeding sections represent the parts of Buchanan and Tullock's book that are most closely related to our current study. But Buchanan and Tullock touched on several other themes. Vote trading, in particular, is traditionally considered one of the central themes in Buchanan and Tullock's work. Buchanan and Tullock analyze a few numerical examples of vote trading under majority rule and draw several conclusions. First, they conclude that there are more advantages to vote trading if individuals receive different benefits from a collective good than if they all receive the same benefit. If they all receive different benefits, members of a minority with intense interests on issue A will have stronger incentive to vote trade with members of a minority with intense interests on issue B than if all members benefit equally.

Second, Buchanan and Tullock argue that under majority rule vote trading can make winning outcomes more efficient. To illustrate the point, they first introduce a simple three-person game without side-payments and show that the solution set depends on which individuals are in the winning coalition. They then compare this result to one with "full" side-payments to show that there can be dramatic improvements in efficiency. They argue that with full side-payments the winning coalition allocates resources to the individuals who benefit the most (whether they are members of the winning coalition or not) and redistribute payments from those who receive the resources to members of the winning coalition in a way that maximizes the return to the winning coalition. Such side-payments may be in dollars or discriminatory taxes on those who receive the good.

For example, Buchanan and Tullock ask use to consider a township with 100 farmers trying to decide which roads to repair (Buchanan and Tullock, 1962, p. 135–9). The first third of the farmers benefit $10 for every dollar spent on the repair of their roads (call these the first coalition), the second third benefit $5 for every dollar spent on the repair of their roads (the second coalition), and the last third benefit $1 for every dollar spent on their roads (the third coalition). To keep the example simple, assume that the marginal productivity of road repair is constant and the township receives a $33 grant to pay for road repairs. If a winning coalition forms between all members of the third coalition and eighteen members of the second coalition, the winning coalition will not allocate road repair to their own roads. Instead, they will allocate road repair to the most productive allocation — the members of the first coalition — and require the first coalition to transfer just less than $10 per member to the winning coalition. Buchanan and Tullock conclude that such side-payments assure that funds will be invested in the most productive manner (to those who value them most) and that gains are shared more symmetrically in terms of benefits than if there were no side-payments. They claim this is true even if the actual allocation of road repairs is nonsymmetric (Buchanan and Tullock, 1962, pp. 154–5).[7]

Although they do not offer formal examples of vote trading, Buchanan and Tullock argue that vote trading produces an outcome between the two extremes of no side-payments and full side payments (Buchanan and Tullock, 1962, p. 155). For them, vote trading is simply an indirect means of making side-payments (Buchanan and Tullock, 1962, p. 156).

Buchanan and Tullock also analyze bicameralism and claim that bicameralism may be an effective means of reducing expected external costs without incurring too many decision making costs (1962, p. 236). Such institutions add to the breath of their analysis but also add to the complexity of decisions expected from individuals at the constitutional stage.

2.5 Conclusion

The *The Calculus of Consent* was one of the first economic studies of constitutional formation. Its recurring themes of decision costs, external costs, and Pareto efficiency were simple, and they had an effect on future studies. Since it was written, social scientists have asked questions about what causes a nation to seek a new constitution (Greif and Laitin, 2004), how constitutions are made (Lijphart, 1999; McGuire, 2003), and what factors allow for corruption in constitutional decision making (Shleifer and Treisman, 2001; Laffont, 2000). They have also re-examined the efficiency of governmental institutions throughout history (North and Weingast, 1989) and studied conditions that allow democracies to succeed (Przeworski, 2005; Lijphart, 1999; Lipset, 1963). These studies have been combined with more traditional themes in public choice about the effects of logrolling (Riker and Brams, 1973), bicameralism (Riker, 1992; Diermeier and Myerson, 1999), agenda setting

---

[7] For a criticism of the generality of these claims see Riker and Brams (1973).

(Koford, 1982), and legislative size (Crain and Tollison, 1977; Dougherty and Edward, 2009).

Because *The Calculus of Consent* had such broad effects on a wide range of research questions, we have found it useful to to revisit some of its central themes. Many of them may now seem commonplace, but only because Buchanan and Tullock made them so. Before we examine these themes carefully, we must first define terms and examine the relationship between unanimity rule and several Pareto concepts. This shows that simple ideas such as the apparently close relationship between unanimity rule and Pareto improvements may not be as close as they seem.

Chapter 3
Clarifying Concepts

3.1 Definitions

Unanimity rule and the Pareto criterion appear so alike that several authors have treated them as almost interchangeable. Arrow (1951) described the Pareto principle as a unanimity principle. Fishburn (1973) refers to the Pareto criterion as strong unanimity. And Buchanan (1967, 285) described unanimity rule as the "political counterpart" of the Pareto criterion.

There are two goals of this chapter. One is to to carefully distinguish different types of unanimity rule from various Pareto concepts. This requires some technical precision that is not necessary for understanding the entire book. Another goal is to discuss the Pareto principles that might be used to judge institutions, including the potential limitation of applying the Pareto criterion to the evaluation of institutions in large populations.

To begin, let N be the number of individuals in a group, committee, or voting population and M be the smallest majority of those individuals; so that $M = (N+1)/2$ for N odd and $M = (N+2)/2$ for N even. Each individual will have preferences over a set of alternatives $\{w,x,y,z,q\}$. We will reserve the term q for the alternative that is also the status quo (i.e., the existing policy, candidate, or state of affairs). For every pair of alternatives $\{x,y\}$, each individual has one of three preferences: $x \succ_i y$ if and only if he/she strictly prefers x to y; $y \succ_i x$ if and only if he/she strictly prefers y to x; and $x \sim_i y$ if and only if he/she is indifferent between the two alternatives.

A list of individual preferences can be summarized in a voter profile. For example, in the three-person voter profile $(x \succ_1 y, y \succ_2 x, x \sim_3 y)$ individual 1 prefers x to y; individual 2 prefers y to x; and individual 3 is indifferent between the two alternatives. Individual preferences can also be summarized in a spatial map, as done in the next chapter.

Two classes of k-majority rule have been used in practice (Dougherty and Edward, 2004).[1] They differ in their treatment of those who "do not vote" and those who vote "abstain."

Definition 3.1. *Absolute k-majority rule*: alternative x defeats the status quo, q, by absolute k-majority rule if and only if $\#yeas \geq k$, where $1 \leq k \leq N$; otherwise q is chosen.

Three common procedures from the absolute class are (1) absolute majority rule (where $k = M$), (2) absolute supermajority rule (where $M < k < N$), and (3) absolute unanimity rule (where $k = N$). Examples from this category include: the U.S. Supreme court requiring the assent of four of its nine justices to grant a writ of certiorari ($k < M$); the majority needed to pass proposals in the Russian Duma ($k = M$); and the ratification of amendments under the Articles of Confederation (which required unanimous consent of all thirteen states). All of these cases determine the winner based on a predetermined threshold of affirmative votes. As a result, they treat responses from those who "do not vote" and those who vote "abstain" the same way as they treat votes against the proposal.

Definition 3.2. *Simple k-majority rule*: alternative x defeats the status quo, q, by simple k-majority rule if and only if $\frac{\#yeas}{\#yeas + \#nays} > k/N$; otherwise q is chosen.

Three common rules from the simple class are simple majority rule in which a proposal passes if the yeas exceed the nays ($k/N = .5$), simple supermajority rule (where $.5 < k/N < 1$), and simple unanimity rule in which a proposal passes if someone votes in favor of it and no one votes opposed ($k/N = 1$). Examples from this class include the simple majority required to pass statutes in most legislatures, such as the U.S. House of Representatives; the two thirds of U.S. Senate needed to convict a U.S. President of impeachment; and the simple unanimity required among permanent members of the U.N. Security Council for nonprocedural decisions.[2]

The absolute and simple class of k-majority rule differ in their treatment of abstentions. Absolute k-majority rule tallies affirmative votes and implicitly treats "do not votes" and "votes to abstain" the same as votes against the proposal. Simple k-majority rule compares the ratio of affirmative votes to negative votes and implicitly ignores "do not votes" and "votes to abstain" in the tally. For any fixed k, if "do not votes" and "votes to abstain" exist, then the simple class is more likely to pass a proposal than the absolute class. When everyone votes and "votes to abstain" are not allowed, the two procedures select equivalently. It is not entirely clear which k-majority rule Buchanan and Tullock attempted to study.

Technical distinctions, such as these, can help us understand subtleties in the relationship between unanimity rule and various Pareto concepts.

---

[1] The terms "absolute" k-majority rule and "simple" k-majority rule are direct extensions of Riker (1982, pp. 44–5). Sen (1979a, pp. 71, 181) makes a similar distinction but uses different nomenclature.

[2] See Laruelle and Valenciano (2010) for additional variants of k-majority rule that have been used in practice.

Definition 3.3. *Pareto criterion*: For any two alternatives x and y, x is Pareto preferred to y if and only if it makes at least one individual better off than y and no individual worse off than y (Sen, 1979a, p. 21).

Definition 3.4. *Weak Pareto criterion*: For any two alternatives x and y, x is weakly Pareto preferred to y if and only if everyone strictly prefers x to y (Arrow, 1951; Sen, 1979b).

Definition 3.5. *BT Criterion*: Proposal x is BT preferred to status quo q if and only if it is Pareto preferred to q; otherwise q is BT preferred to x (Buchanan and Tullock, 1962; Head, 1974; Rogowski, 1974; Tsebelis, 1990).

It is important to note that Buchanan and Tullock (1962), Head (1974), and Rogowski (1974) refer to Definition 3.5 as the Pareto criterion.[3] Tsebelis (1990, p. 104) refers to Definition 3.5 as the "efficiency" criterion. However, Definition 3.5 clearly differs from Definition 3.3, and needs to be treated separately. We refer to it as the BT criterion in honor of Buchanan and Tullock.[4]

Definition 3.6. *Pareto optimality*: Alternative x is Pareto optimal if there does not exist an alternative y that is Pareto preferred to x (Sen, 1979a).

For any two alternatives x and y, x is "Pareto preferred" (or Pareto superior) to y if it adheres to Definition 3.3; x is "Pareto dispreferred" (or Pareto inferior) to y if y is Pareto preferred to x; and the two alternatives are "Pareto indeterminate" if neither x is Pareto preferred to y nor y is Pareto preferred to x. Throughout the book we will use the notation $PP(y)$ to refer to any alternative that is Pareto preferred to y; $PD(y)$ to refer to any alternative that is Pareto dispreferred to y, and PO to refer to any alternative that is Pareto optimal. Note that Pareto optimality is not conditioned upon any particular alternative. Points that are not Pareto optimal are called Pareto sub-optimal.

Finally, we define neutrality to help us understand the relationship between several concepts.

Definition 3.7. *Neutrality*: If x defeats (ties) y for one preference profile and all individuals have the same ordinal rankings for z and w as they have for x and y (i.e. $x \succeq_j y \rightarrow z \succeq_i w$, and so on), then z defeats (ties) w (Mueller, 2003, p. 134).

Neutrality suggests that voting rules, and other institutions, should not favor one of the alternatives irrespective of individual preferences for that alternative. Whatever criterion permits us to say that x is socially as good as y should also be sufficient for declaring that y is socially as good as x if everyone reverses their preferences.

---

[3] Sen (1979a, p. 25), Berggren (1996, pp. 339–40), and Buchanan (1962) interpret Buchanan and Tullock's criterion as we do. Buchanan and Tullock claim that a desirable change can be made "only if all persons agree" (Buchanan and Tullock, 1962, pp. 92–3). That is, only if *everyone* is made better off.

[4] See Dougherty and Edward (2004, 2010a) for applications of the BT criterion.

3.2 Pareto Preference

Although the differences between the Pareto criterion (Definition 3.3) and the BT criterion (Definition 3.5) may appear subtle, the two criteria can evaluate sets of individual preferences quite differently. This is because the Pareto criterion maintains neutrality with respect to the status quo while the BT criterion favors the status quo. For example, in the three-person voter profile $(x \succ_1 q, x \succ_2 q, q \succ_3 x)$, neither alternative is Pareto preferred to the other. The Pareto criterion makes an indeterminate judgement (i.e., does not recommend one alternative over the other), while the BT criterion recommends the status quo. If Pareto indeterminate cases are likely, then the two criteria will often judge outcomes differently.

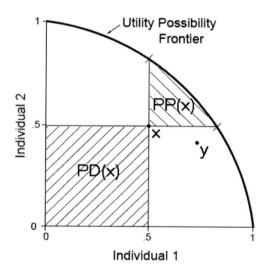

Fig. 3.1 Pareto Preference vs. Pareto Indeterminance

The difference can be illustrated with the help of Figure 3.1. This figure depicts the set of possible utility levels for two individuals, normalized to $(0, 1)$. The utility possibility frontier (top right edge of the figure) plots the maximum attainable utility given the resources and technology available at the time.

Consider point x. Points to the top-right of x, inclusive of points on the vertical and horizontal lines through .5, are Pareto preferred to x because they make at least one individual better off and no one worse off. These points are indicated by the shaded area marked $PP(x)$. Points to the bottom left of x, inclusive of points on the dotted line, are Pareto dispreferred to x because x is Pareto preferred to each point in this area. These points are indicated by the shaded area marked $PD(x)$. Points in the unshaded regions under the utility possibility frontier (i.e., those top-left and bottom-right of x) are Pareto indeterminate with respect to x.

Now suppose x is the status quo. Both the Pareto criterion (Definition 3.3) and the BT criterion (Definition 3.5) judge alternatives top-right of x as something preferred to x. However, the criteria make different judgements about the alternatives in the unshaded areas. If x is the status quo and y is the proposal, then alternative x is not Pareto preferred to y, nor is y Pareto preferred to x. In this sense, the two alternatives are Pareto indeterminate because the Pareto criterion (Definition 3.3) makes no judgment about the pair. The BT criterion, in contrast, suggests that x should be preferred to y because if neither alternative is Pareto preferred to the other, then the status quo, x, should be judged preferable according to the BT criterion. Sen (1979a) refers to such a criterion as a Pareto extension rule because it makes a judgement in cases where the Pareto criterion does not.

Clearly, the Pareto criterion is neutral and the BT criterion is non-neutral. If y were the status quo, the Pareto criterion would make the same indeterminate judgement. However, the BT criterion would now prefer y because in the absence of Pareto preferred alternatives, the BT criterion always favors the status quo. Hence, the status quo plays an important role in the BT criterion.

3.3 Pareto Optimality

Figure 3.1 also demonstrates the concept of Pareto optimality. Any point on the utility possibility frontier is considered Pareto optimal because an individual's utility cannot be improved without reducing the utility of the other individual. This includes any point on the arc. Points inside the frontier are considered Pareto suboptimal because for each of these points there exists at least one point that makes at least one individual better off without making the other individual worse off.

Now since there is a concept of Pareto optimality, one might think there should be a concept of "BT optimality." However, it seems impossible to define BT optimality because the BT criterion requires the status quo to be one of the two points of comparison.[5]

Nevertheless, there are refinements to Pareto optimality that may capture much of the same sentiment. For example, if scholars want to guarantee that an outcome is both Pareto optimal and a Pareto improvement from the status quo, then they should be interested in the intersection of the set of alternatives Pareto preferred to the status quo and the alternatives that are Pareto optimal. If x is the status quo in

---

[5] Suppose a point x was defined as "BT optimal" if there did not exist an alternative y that is BT preferred to x. Now consider a point x' that is fixed on the utility possibility frontier. There are four conditions of q that affect the status of x'. First, if $q = x'$, then x' would be the only BT optimal alternative. Second, if $q \neq x'$ but q is on the utility possibility frontier, then x' would not be BT optimal; q would. Third, if $q \neq x'$ and q is interior to the utility possibility frontier (i.e. Pareto suboptimal), then we cannot determine whether x' is BT optimal. No alternatives are BT preferred to x', but x' is not the status quo, so no BT judgement can be made between x' and alternatives that are not Pareto preferred to x', with the exception of q. Fourth, if q does not exist, as in an open seat election, then BT comparisons cannot be made and again the concept of BT optimality would be poorly defined.

Figure 3.1, then the set of alternatives that are $PP(x)\&PO$ are the set of points on the utility possibility frontier between the two hash marks. Such points make at least one of the two individuals better off without hurting the other and they exhaust the possibility of additional Pareto improvements.

Both Pareto optimality and Pareto optimality combined with Pareto superiority to the status quo have been used to evaluate policies and institutions in the literature. For example, the common pool resource and public goods literatures typically focus on Pareto optimal outcomes that are also Pareto improvements from the initial status quo (Ostrom, 1990; Cornes and Sandler, 1996; Mueller, 2003, pp. 67–72; Weimer and Vining, 2005, p. 56). In these cases, it is important for policy makers to know whether voluntary contribution is an improvement from the initial contribution of no one contributing as well as to determine if Pareto improvements have been exhausted.

For example, Lindahl ([1919] 1967) had this concept in mind when he wrote his theory on just taxation. Lindahl argued that if individuals voted on the financing of public goods using unanimity rule then they would select a quantity of the public good and a distribution of the costs that was both Pareto optimal and a Pareto improvement from the status quo of not having the public good.[6] In this case, the combination of Pareto superiority and Pareto optimality make sense because there is a reasonable status quo from which Pareto superiority can be judged — the status quo of no public good provided.[7]

Other scholars have evaluated institutions using Pareto optimality without restricting their attention to outcomes that are also Pareto superior to the status quo. This is common in the social choice and legislative decision making literatures (Arrow, 1951; Sen, 1979a; Nurmi, 1987; Aldrich, 1995; Colomer, 2001; Tsebelis, 2002; Mueller, 2003, pp. 138–43; Austen-Smith and Banks 2005). In these cases, the status quo does not have a special position because scholars want to make decisions neutrally (i.e., based solely on welfare) or because the status quo is just one of many alternatives, such as the policy of the previous regime, that should not have undue influence on the judgement of the outcome. Of course, in endorsing Pareto optimality such scholars may or may not value every Pareto optimal outcome equally. They may simply want to avoid outcomes that are not Pareto efficient as a first cut.

For example, Aldrich (1995) studies whether majority rule coalitions, universal coalitions, or pluralistic coalitions are Pareto optimal. He does not consider whether they are Pareto improvements from the status quo because the status quo is arbitrary. Aldrich applies a divide the dollar game to his study of party formation in the U.S. legislature. In this game, there are three, two-person coalitions (or parties) that could exist. From a formal theoretic perspective, the first two-person coalition to form is entirely arbitrary. Hence, evaluating "fair" institutions as Pareto improvements from a two-person coalition that happened to exist in the previous period might be arbitrary as well. Perhaps this is why Aldrich judges institutions using Pareto optimality without the additional restriction of Pareto superiority to the status quo.

---

[6] Lindahl's suggestion had problems, such as not being compatible with an accurate revelation of preferences.

[7] See (Grafstein, 1990) for an interesting discussion of unanimity rule and the status quo.

Buchanan and Tullock seem to favor institutional changes that are Pareto improvements to the status quo. However, Buchanan also make statements such as "[i]t is evident that [unanimous consent] is the political counterpart of the Pareto criterion for optimality" (Buchanan, 1967, p. 285).[8] We examine both criteria for completeness. Although we will discuss these criteria in Chapter 4 and the conclusion, we leave it for the reader to decide which criterion is more appropriate for constitutional and legislative decision making.

3.4 Unanimity Rule and the Pareto Principles

Even though some authors use terms like unanimity rule and the Pareto criterion synonymously (Buchanan, 1967; Fishburn, 1973; Weimer and Vining, 2005, p. 160; Dietrich and List, 2007), it now should be clear that neither class of unanimity rule (absolute or simple) is equivalent to the Pareto criterion (Definition 3.3). There are several reasons.

First, both unanimity rules select alternatives based on actions (such as the decision to vote and which alternative to vote for). The Pareto criterion evaluates alternatives based on the preferences of both voters and nonvoters. For example, if there are three individuals, all three prefer x to q, and all three do not vote (perhaps due to the rationality of voting), then both unanimity rules will select the status quo while the Pareto criterion will favor the proposal.

Second, both unanimity rules differ from the Pareto criterion in terms of neutrality. For example, suppose all individuals vote and they vote sincerely. That is, they vote for their true preferences on every pairwise comparison of alternatives. Then in the three person voter profile ($x \succ_1 q$, $x \succ_2 q$, $q \succ_3 x$) both unanimity rules select the status quo while the Pareto criterion remains indeterminate between the two alternatives.

Third, absolute unanimity rule differs from the Pareto criterion in its treatment of indifference. In the voter profile ($x \succ_1 q, x \succ_2 q, x \sim_3 q$), if all three voters turnout and vote sincerely (voter three calls out "abstain"), then absolute unanimity rule selects the status quo even though the proposal is Pareto preferred.

Furthermore, neither class of unanimity rule is equivalent to the weak Pareto criterion (Definition 3.4). Again there are three reasons. First, as in the previous case, both unanimity rules select based on the action of voters. The weak Pareto criterion recommends alternatives based on preferences. Second, even if all individuals vote and they vote sincerely, both unanimity rules violate neutrality, while the weak Pareto criterion is neutral with respect to the two alternatives. Third, in contrast to the previous case, both absolute unanimity rule and simple unanimity

---

[8] Buchanan and Tullock (1962, p. 172) describe a "social state" as Pareto optimal similar to our Definition 3.6. However, on the bottom of the same page they classify *changes* as Pareto optimal if they make Pareto improvements. They then write "a change from A to G is Pareto-optimal in itself, although it represents a shift from one nonoptimal position to another" (p. 174). Such statements seem to mix the concepts of Pareto optimality and Pareto improvements.

rule differ from the weak Pareto criterion in their treatment of indifference. In the profile $(x \succ_1 q, x \succ_2 q, x \sim_3 q)$, for example, if all individuals turn out and vote sincerely, absolute unanimity rule selects the status quo, simple unanimity rule selects the proposal, and the weak Pareto criterion makes an indeterminate judgement.

If we define the two unanimity rules neutrally, in an attempt to make them more like Definitions 3.3 and 3.4, then neither voting rule will be decisive. A second stage, such as flipping a coin, will be needed to determine the outcome whenever there is no consensus. Defining unanimity rule neutrally is further discouraged by the fact that no examples of such a rule appear in practice.

If we define the Pareto criterion non-neutrally, in an attempt to make it more like simple unanimity rule, then we get the BT criterion (Definition 3.5). If everyone votes and votes sincerely, then the BT criterion and simple unanimity rule are equivalent in pair-wise votes. However, absolute unanimity rule and the BT criterion are not equivalent because they differ in their treatment of indifference. In the case of $(x \succ_1 q, x \succ_2 q, x \sim_3 q)$, for example, absolute unanimity rule selects the status quo while the BT criterion recommends the proposal.

Finally, it should be fairly obvious that neither version of unanimity rule is equivalent to Pareto optimality because the definition of Pareto optimality deals with the nonexistence of a set of Pareto preferred alternatives, while unanimity rule makes choices between two alternatives.[9]

3.5 Pareto Indeterminance

Our next task is to show why these subtle differences are important for medium- and large-sized populations. To do this, assume that preferences are randomly drawn from the domain of all possible preferences and that each of the pairwise rankings between any x and y $(x \succ_i q, x \sim_i q,$ and $q \succ_i x)$ occur in the domain with probabilities p_1, p_0, and p_{-1}, respectively.[10] These probabilities reflect uncertainty about preferences, which institutional framers would have if they select voting rules before actors or alternatives are fully known.

For future chapters it will be useful to note that the homogeneity of a population can affect these probabilities. In a homogenous population, proposals will tend to be either uniformly liked or uniformly disliked. If a proposer tends to propose

---

[9] Furthermore, if the universe of alternatives contained only two elements, with at least one individual favoring the status quo and at least one other individual favoring the proposal, then both the status quo and the proposal would be Pareto optimal. Both unanimity rules, in contrast, would chose the status quo.

[10] For simplicity, we assume that each individual has the same preference probabilities and that these probabilities are independent. One way to meet these two assumptions is to randomly draw an assembly from a meta-population. For example, a Board of Education randomly drawn from a conservative county may prefer school vouchers to the status quo of publicly funded education with probabilities $p_1 = .60$, $p_0 = .10$, and $p_{-1} = .30$, while a Board of Education drawn from a liberal county may prefer the two alternatives with probabilities $p_1 = .30$, $p_0 = .10$, and $p_{-1} = .60$. Stochastic preferences might also assure independence.

something in line with their individual or group interests, then p_1 will be large and p_{-1} will be small. In a heterogenous population, a proposer might find it difficult to formulate successful proposals. In other words, p_1 will be small and p_{-1} will be large.

Proposition 1 *If $p_1, p_{-1} > 0$, then Pr(Pareto indeterminacy) $\rightarrow$ 1, as $N \rightarrow \infty$.*

Proof. The probability of Pareto indeterminacy is:

$$1 - (p_1 + p_0)^N - (p_{-1} + p_0)^N + p_0^N. \tag{3.1}$$

Since $p_1, p_{-1} > 0$ it follows that $(p_1 + p_0) < 1$, $(p_{-1} + p_0) < 1$, and $p_0 < 1$; therefore $(p_1 + p_0)^N \rightarrow 0$, $(p_{-1} + p_0)^N \rightarrow 0$, and $p_0^N \rightarrow 0$ as $N \rightarrow \infty$. $\square$

Although Proposition 1 is stated for infinite populations, for all intents and purposes the formula for the probability of Pareto indeterminacy (cases where neither x is Pareto preferred to q nor q is Pareto preferred to x) converges to 1 in much smaller populations (see Table 3.1). For example, if $p_1 = p_{-1} = 1/2$, then the probability of Pareto indeterminacy approximates 1 at $N = 8$. If $p_1 = .95$, $p_0 = .02$, $p_{-1} = .03$, then the probability of Pareto indeterminacy approximates 1 at $N = 138$. Even if everyone is extremely likely prefer the motion, Definition 3.3 is expected to make no judgement in populations the size of the U.S. House of Representatives, a town, or a small city (areas where the Pareto criterion is supposed to help make judgements about constitutional designs).

Table 3.1 Sizes of N where the probability of Pareto indeterminacy $\simeq 1$

Preference Probabilities p_1, p_0, p_{-1}	Converges at
0.50, 0.00, 0.50	$N = 8$
0.70, 0.05, 0.25	$N = 16$
0.90, 0.05, 0.05	$N = 90$
0.95, 0.02, 0.03	$N = 138$
0.03, 0.02, 0.95	$N = 138$

Note: A probability is considered approximately 1 if the unrounded probability differs from 1 by 10^{-2} or less.

Of course, a similar proposition for unanimity rule (simple and absolute) exists. As N approaches infinity, the probability that unanimity rule will select the status quo approaches 1. This implies that in populations the size of the U.S. House of Representatives, a town, or a small city, *unanimity rule will almost certainly select the status quo. The Pareto criterion will almost certainly make no judgement.* Hence, unanimity rule and the Pareto criterion will rarely select the same outcome in subjects of interest to political scientists and social choice theorists. The subtle differences in the definitions imply large differences in practice and give us greater reason to caution against using unanimity rule and the Pareto criterion as synony-mous.[11]

3.5.1 Implications

The implications of Proposition 1 should be obvious. If preferences are indepen-dent, then the Pareto criterion by itself is unlikely to create a complete ordering in judgements of constitutional design, legislative decision making, and popular elec-tions. It will rarely judge between Pareto sub-optimal points, Pareto optimal points, or any two points in these settings. The same is true for the weak Pareto criterion (Definition 3.4).

One response to this indeterminacy is to create a Pareto extension rule that makes the Pareto criterion more complete. For example, Pareto indeterminate cases could be judged in favor of the status quo. This is the implicit approach of the BT cri-terion (Definition 3.5). The problem with this approach is that the new criterion is dominated by the extension rule, not by Pareto criterion itself. Hence, the idea that a constitution, institution, or public good should be adopted only if it produces a Pareto improvement (Buchanan, 1962; Mueller, 2003; Cornes and Sandler, 1996) turns on the justification for the extension rule, not on the welfare patterns that make up the Pareto criterion. For example, scholars who want to preserve the status quo in cases of Pareto indeterminacy to protect individual rights are almost always making a rights-based judgement. They are rarely making judgements implied by the Pareto criterion.

Finally, Proposition 1 can also be interpreted as stating that in large populations with two alternatives, both alternatives are very likely to be Pareto optimal, because Pareto indeterminacy implies that neither alternative is Pareto preferred to the other. In cases with A alternatives, where A is any fixed positive integer, it is easy to extend Proposition 1 and prove the same conclusions. In other words, for sufficiently large populations faced with a finite number of alternatives, all alternatives are very likely to be Pareto optimal.

Of course, if preferences are probabilistically dependent, the probability of Pareto indeterminacy may not increase as rapidly as Table 3.1 suggests. However, the claim that Pareto indeterminacy is likely in large populations may still apply. For example, in the spatial voting models introduced in the next chapter, individ-ual preferences over a set of alternatives are probabilistically dependent. However, the probability of randomly selecting a Pareto optimal outcome among randomly se-

---

[11] The same point can be seen in the familiar utilities possibility frontier. Suppose the outer edge of Figure 3.1 were flat between $(1,0)$ and $(1,1)$ and vertical between $(0,1)$ and $(1,1)$, so that the area underneath the utilities possibility curve formed a square. In this case, roughly $1/2$ the area would be Pareto indeterminate with respect to $(0.5,0.5)$ — the areas top-left and bottom-right of $(0.5,0.5)$. If we added a third person on a third dimension, roughly $6/8$ of the areas would be Pareto indeterminate with respect to $(0.5,0.5,0.5)$. The illustration extends to N individuals in N dimension, with the probability of Pareto indeterminacy matching that produced by equation (3.1) for $p_1 = p_{-1} = 0.5$.

lected ideal points still increases as N increases. If ideal points are drawn from a uniform distribution on the unit square, if alternatives are drawn from the same distribution, and if individuals prefer alternatives closer to alternatives farther away, then for $N = 99$ an alternative is Pareto optimal roughly 88% of the time. For $N = 200$ an alternative is Pareto optimal roughly 93% of the time. This again suggests that the Pareto criterion may have limited applications in large legislatures and elections. Common types of probabilistic dependence may not save us from the result.

3.6 Conclusion

Although simple unanimity rule is equivalent to the BT criterion if everyone votes sincerely, it is not equivalent to more commonly used Pareto principles such as the Pareto criterion (Definition 3.3) or weak Pareto criterion (Definition 3.4). It is also not equivalent to the BT criterion if individuals vote strategically. Hence, using unanimity rule as a proxy for a Pareto concept can only be justified in limited situations.

The Pareto criterion is a reasonable method for judging a network of small N interactions, such as bilateral trade in a market economy. It can also be compelling for large N interactions as a sufficient condition. That is, if there is a Pareto preferred alternative, society ought to chose it (Arrow, 1951). It is less compelling, however, as a necessary condition, particularly since the Pareto criterion is unlikely to make judgements in medium- and large-sized populations. Pareto indeterminacy, a positive property, simply makes the Pareto criterion too incapable of making normative judgements — particularly if side payments are not allowed. In such cases, making the Pareto criterion necessary implies creating a society which almost always makes no judgements. Nevertheless, we will use this criterion as a *sufficient* condition in Chapters 4 and 5. In the next chapter, we will evaluate k-majority rules in terms of Pareto optimality and the intersection of Pareto optimality and Pareto supremacy to the status quo.

Chapter 4
Constitutional Decision Making

4.1 Introduction

K-majority rules, such as majority rule, supermajority rules, and unanimity rule, have been used in legislative settings. The British House of Commons and the U.S. House of Representatives use simple majority rule for ordinary decisions; the U.S. Senate requires approval of 3/5ths of its members to pass "filibuster-proof" legislation; and the Council of the European Union requires unanimity rule for votes in some issue areas.

At the constitutional stage, framers must decide, among other things, which voting rule is the most appropriate for the legislature. How they might make that choice is particularly perplexing because constitutional framers would be in some type of infinite regress if they voted on the most appropriate voting rule for choosing voting rules. To avoid this problem, the most appropriate voting rule at the constitutional phase is usually based on first principles.

Traditionally, social contract theorists have used the notion of unanimous consent to justify government (Hobbes, [1651] 1962; Locke, [1690] 1988; Rousseau, [1762] 1997). They have claimed that political authority and moral obligation to that authority stems from individual agreement. Without each individual's consent, social contracts might violate the pre-constitutional interests of various individuals. Hence, unanimity might be considered a fair voting rule for helping a nation bootstrap its institutions. More recently, scholars have extended contractarian ideals to the creation of actual constitutions (Buchanan and Tullock, 1962; Mueller, 1996; Hardin, 1999; Brennan and Hamlin, 2000). Most of these scholars agree that the best procedure for creating new constitutions is unanimity rule because without transaction costs, unanimity rule only produces Pareto improvements from the pre-constitutional status quo and Pareto optimal results.[1]

This chapter analyzes which k-majority rule is most desirable for constitutional decision making. In other words, which rule should be used to make decisions about

---

[1] One clear exception is Hardin (1999), who justifies constitutions based on contractarian notions but does not advocate unanimity rule.

the most appropriate voting rule, and other aspects of the institutional design assuming decision making costs, and other transaction costs, are negligible. The relationships developed in this chapter also apply to the choice of the most optimal k-majority rule in a legislature — particularly for cases *without* decision costs. Nevertheless, we will reserve the next chapter, on legislative decision making, for a discussion of optimal k-majority rules *with* decision costs.

More specifically, this chapter examines which k-majority rule(s) is best suited for attaining Pareto preferred and Pareto optimal outcomes, both separately and combined, in a spatial voting model with random proposals, sincere proposals, or strategic proposals. We employ spatial voting models because the traditional spatial voting literature widely supports the notion that unanimity rule is the best voting rule for producing Pareto optimal outcomes that are Pareto preferred to the status quo and/or Pareto optimal. Spatial voting models are perhaps the most widely used formal model in political science and have been used in economics and other disciplines. Hence, they should be accessible to a wide audience. We examine random and sincere proposals because we want to understand the raw properties of the voting rules themselves, not the properties that are unique to certain behavioral assumptions. Such an investigation is analogous to the studies of Becker (1962) and Gode and Sunder (1993) who ask whether a free market can produce Pareto optimal results if individuals lack certain levels of intelligence. To complete our study, we also analyze strategic behavior — the most common assumption about human behavior in the study of politics and economics.

We report three striking results related to Pareto optimality, which are largely extensions of Dougherty and Edward (2005, 2010b). First, if proposal generation is random and voting is sincere, then majority rule is usually more likely to select a Pareto optimal outcome than unanimity rule. This is true for various distributions of ideal points and alternatives, as well as single and multidimensional issue spaces. Second, if individuals propose and vote sincerely, then majority rule selects Pareto optimal outcomes at least as well as unanimity rule. Third, if individuals propose and vote strategically, then unanimity rule will always yield a Pareto optimal outcome. Other k-majority rules will often yield a Pareto optimal outcome, and will always yield an outcome that is very close to Pareto optimal.

We also compare the various k-majority rules in their likelihood of delivering an outcome which is Pareto preferred to the initial status quo, and in their likelihood of delivering an outcome that is both Pareto preferred to the initial status quo *and* Pareto optimal. We find that unanimity rule is at least as likely to select Pareto preferred outcomes as other k-majority rules. And with some exceptions for random proposing, unanimity rule is at least as likely as majority rule to select a Pareto optimal outcome that is also Pareto preferred to the initial status quo.

Hence, if good constitutional decision making should strive for outcomes that are both Pareto optimal and Pareto superior to the pre-constitutional status quo, then unanimity rule is the best voting rule for producing Pareto optimal results. Our results formalize and corroborate this widely held conjecture. If Pareto superiority to the initial status quo is not required, then Pareto optimal voting may not require consensus. Instead, majority rule may be more capable of producing Pareto efficient constitutional designs, public goods, and policy decisions than unanimity rule. Such first principles should be of interest to those who relate unanimity rule to Pareto principles in the study of political parties (Aldrich, 1995), legislative institutions (Niou and Ordeshook, 1985; Colomer, 2001), separation of powers games (Hammond and Miller, 1987; Miller and Hammond, 1990; Tsebelis, 2002), and public goods (Lindahl, [1919] 1967; Cornes and Sandler, 1996), and most importantly constitutional design.

4.1.1 Notation

To focus the study, consider N individuals each with an ideal point I_i in an n-dimensional space that is bounded and closed on a hyper-square. Each individual has single peaked and symmetric utility, which implies they prefer alternatives closer to their ideal point more than alternatives farther away. Further assume no transactions costs (such as decision making costs),[2] no vote trading, and, unless we specify otherwise, indifferent voters will abstain.

Although several of the results described in this chapter apply to any number of dimensions, we focus on one or two dimensions in our examples. Two or more dimensions of alternatives tend to produce qualitatively different results than a single dimension of alternatives (McKelvey, 1976; Schofield, 1978). In a single dimension, the median voter is well defined, intransitivity cannot occur if preferences are single peaked, and alternatives closer to the median defeat alternatives farther away (Hinich and Munger, 1997). Furthermore, the majority rule and unanimity rule cores are Pareto optimal in a single dimension. Alternative x is an element of the unanimity rule core (resp. majority rule core) if there does not exist another alternative y that a unanimity (resp. majority) of individuals prefer to x. In other words, traditionally viewed, all k-majority rules should produce some Pareto optimal result in equilibrium. This is not the case for multidimensional spaces. In two, or more, dimensions a median is no longer defined, intransitivities are common under majority rule, and the majority rule core is typically empty. This makes it more difficult to see why majority rule would produce Pareto optimal results in two or more dimensions. Hence, we will focus on the more difficult, two-dimensional case in many of our examples.

Voting proceeds in our analysis using a forward agenda. In other words, the initial status quo q_1 is paired against a proposal x_1 in round 1. The winning alternative in round 1 is then paired against a new proposal x_2 in round 2, x_r in round r, and so on, for a total of R rounds. For $r > 1$, q_r indicates the status quo in round r, i.e., the winning proposal from round $(r-1)$. In what follows, we will refer to both the proposal and the corresponding point in space as x_r (similarly for q_r). Forward agendas are

---

[2] It is easy to confuse behavior from nonrational proposals and no transaction costs (our first setting) with behavior from rational proposals, complete information, and no transaction costs (Dougherty and Edward, 2010b). The latter would always produce a Pareto preferred proposal under unanimity rule if the status quo was suboptimal. *A priori* the former may not.

consistent with Tullock's (1998, pp. 70–4) and Mueller's (2003) description of how unanimity rule should produce Pareto optimal results. A fixed number of rounds helps assure that everything else is held equal except the voting rule we manipulate. It would also result from rules that limit the number of amendments, enact time limitations, or create backward agendas.[3] All of which are common in deliberative assemblies.

Although constitutional political economists and social contract theorists typically think in terms of absolute unanimity rule which passes proposals if and only if #\{yeas\} = N, this chapter will focus on the *simple k-majority rule* for three reasons. First, simple k-majority rules are more common in practice. Second, simple k-majority rules are weaker than absolute k-majority rules. Hence, the results presented here apply to both classes. Third, indifference occurs with a probability of roughly zero in spatial voting models. If everyone votes and there are no "votes to abstain," then the alternative chosen under any absolute k-majority rule and the equivalent simple k-majority rule will often be the same. We will refer to simple majority rule and simple unanimity rule as majority rule and unanimity rule (resp.) for the remainder of this chapter.

Furthermore, we will use the notation $PP(q_1)$ to refer to any alternative that is Pareto preferred (i.e., Pareto superior) to q_1 and $PP(q_1)\&PO$ to refer to any outcome that is both Pareto preferred to the initial status quo q_1 and Pareto optimal. The sets of alternatives that meet both properties are easy to define in a spatial model.

4.2 Pareto Principles in a Spatial Context

To make the arguments in this chapter easier to follow, we will use the U.S. Constitutional Convention as a running example. At the convention delegates voted in state blocs, with the majority of a delegation determining the vote for a delegate's state. A simple majority of the states determined whether a motion carried. We make no attempt to recover the location of delegates at the Constitutional Convention, largely because we want to avoid the complication of bloc voting but also because it is difficult to infer the position of all delegates. Instead we treat states as unitary actors and consider the effect of various k-majority rules on these twelve unitary actors as an illustrative example.[4]

Since we are not trying to carefully resolve arguments about the proper location of states, we estimated both a single-dimensional mapping of state ideal points and and a two-dimensional mapping of state ideal points from using a 35×528 roll call matrix and w-nominate software (http://voteview.com/w-nominate.htm). W-nominate assumes delegates have symmetric utility functions consisting of probabilistic utility component that is a function of the distance between the delegate and a roll call outcome (proposal or status quo), and a stochastic idiosyncratic com-

---

[3] In a backward agenda individuals propose alternatives $x_1, ..., x_r$ and the voting proceeds x_r against x_{r-1}, winner against x_{r-2}, etc., with the last remaining proposal matched against the status quo, q_1.

[4] There were thirteen states in the confederation, but Rhode Island never sent a delegation.

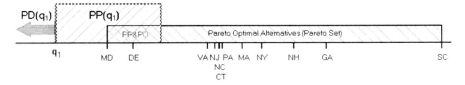

Fig. 4.1 A Single Dimensional Estimate of State Positions at the U.S. Constitutional Convention

ponent which is modeled as random draw from a logit distribution. W-nominate estimates legislator ideal points and roll call outcomes that maximize the joint probability of the votes. For other estimates of state locations at the Constitutional Convention, see Jillson (1988), Dougherty and Heckelman (2006), and Pope and Treier (2009). For estimates of delegate locations see Heckelman and Dougherty (2010b).

Twelve of the rows in our matrix are for the states that attended the Constitutional Convention. An additional thirteen rows are for the thirteen states that voted in Congress when the Articles of Confederation were formed (June 7, 1776 – December 31, 1777). The remaining nine rows are for all the delegates who voted in both assemblies during these periods. The columns include 64 motions from the creation of the Articles of Confederation (31 of which were not directly related to the clauses of the Articles) and 464 motions from the Constitutional Convention.[5] In both cases a motion was included only if at least one state was recorded as a yea and at least one other state was recorded as a nay. Although delegate information is discarded, we include delegates who voted during both periods in the roll call matrix to provide some overlap in the data and to allow each state to have two separate locations. This allows us to make make conjectures about the location of the status quo prior to the Constitutional Convention later in this chapter.

A single-dimensional estimate of state ideal points at the Constitutional Convention appears in Figure 4.1. State labels appear underneath the dimension, along with a hypothetical initial status quo q_1. Since delegates from New Hampshire and New York never attended at the same time, Connecticut is most accurately characterized as the median voter. However, to keep the exposition simple, we presume that all twelve states attended simultaneously.

Figure 4.1 illustrates several of the concepts defined in the previous chapter. The alternatives Pareto dispreferred to the initial status quo q_1, $PD(q_1)$, are all the alternatives to the left of q_1 as well as alternatives sufficiently to the right (not shown).[6] The alternatives Pareto preferred to q_1 range from q_1 to Maryland, the closest state, and the same distance to the right of Maryland. This interval is marked by right diagonal shading and $PP(q_1)$. In a spatial voting model with Euclidean preferences, the set of Pareto *optimal* points is the convex hull of the ideal points, including al-

---

[5] Data for state votes from August 8, 1777 to December 31, 1777 came from Lord (1984). Data for state votes from the Constitutional Convention came from Farrand (1966). The remaining state votes and delegate votes were inferred as part of a grant, funded by the National Science Foundation, SES-0752098, Keith Dougherty and Jac Heckelman principle investigators.

[6] These alternatives are at least as great as SC + |SC − q_1|.

ternatives on the edges of the hull. In our single-dimensional model, this is the set of alternatives from the actor furthest left, Maryland, to the actor furthest right, South Carolina.

The set of Pareto optimal alternatives are indicated by left diagonal shading. As commonly done in the literature (Ordeshook, 1986; Austen-Smith and Banks, 2005; Duggan, 2006), we will refer to this set as the Pareto set throughout this book. For any set of ideal points, the Pareto set remains fixed, but the set of Pareto preferred alternatives and the set of Pareto dispreferred alternatives vary by the location of the alternative it is compared against (in our case, the status quo). If q_r were in the Pareto set, then the set of alternatives Pareto preferred to q_r would be empty.

Two-dimensional estimates of the states at the U.S. Constitutional Convention are displayed in Figure 4.2. Here, the first dimension is largely correlated with various powers of the national government, while the second dimension shows some divide between Northern and Southern states. The figure also displays the familiar small state coalition on the top-middle of the figure and the large state coalition toward the middle-right of the figure.[7]

Again, the figure can help us clarify several of the concepts defined in the previous chapter. For the status quo depicted in Figure 4.2, the set of Pareto dispreferred points are all the points in the dark shaded area on the bottom left-hand side of the figure (inclusive). Pareto preferred points are indicated by the lens-shaped area with right diagonal shading (inclusive). The boundary of both are determined by indifference curves of the actors at the extremes, Delaware and South Carolina. All alternatives outside one of these two sets are Pareto indeterminate to q_1. These alternatives are neither Pareto preferred to q_1, nor Pareto dispreferred to q_1 — a large area in the figure. The set of Pareto optimal alternatives, the Pareto set, is depicted in the top-right of the figure with left diagonal shading. In this case, the set of alternatives Pareto preferred to q_1 covers a large portion of the Pareto set, but there are elements of the $PP(q_1)$ set that are not Pareto optimal.

4.2.1 The Spatial Voting Literature

The claim that unanimity rule is the best voting rule for producing Pareto preferred and Pareto optimal outcomes is reinforced by the spatial voting literature.

To illustrate the claim that unanimity rule is particularly adept at producing Pareto preferred outcomes consider an example from Figure 4.1. In this case, if all individuals vote sincerely, the only alternatives that can pass under unanimity rule are those closer to the left pivot (Maryland) than they are to the initial status quo,

---

[7] The large state coalition consisted of Georgia, Massachusetts, North Carolina, Pennsylvania, South Carolina, and Virginia. Georgia and North Carolina are traditionally considered part of the the large state coalition because they anticipated population growth in their western districts and voted with that group (Jillson, 1978). Delegates from New Hampshire arrived at the convention after most of the debate on apportionment was complete. This may explain why New Hampshire is oddly positioned closer to the large state coalition.

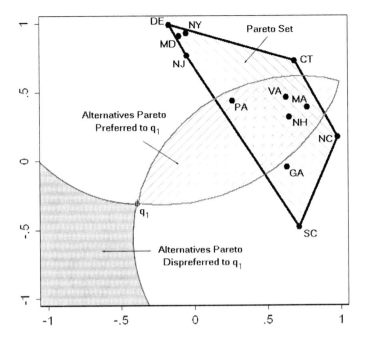

Fig. 4.2 Two-Dimensional Estimates of State Positions at the U.S. Constitutional Convention

q_1. This is equivalent to the set of alternatives Pareto preferred to q_1. If, in contrast, the decision was made under majority rule, then a majority of states might pass an alternative that made other states worse off, as in the move from q_1 to *VA* in Figure 4.1. This move would produce a Pareto indeterminate outcome.

In the two-dimensional case (Figure 4.2), the only alternatives that can pass under unanimity rule are the alternatives in the right-shaded area, which is the set of alternatives Pareto preferred to q_1. If the decision was made under majority rule, then a majority of states might pass an alternative such as the point at South Carolina's ideal point. The change would make other states, Delaware, Maryland, and New Jersey, worse off. Again, q_1 and SC are Pareto indeterminate.

Now consider the relationship between unanimity rule and Pareto optimality. Under unanimity rule, all points in the Pareto set are in the unanimity rule core, and all points in the unanimity rule core must be in the Pareto set, regardless of the dimensions of the policy space (Ordeshook, 1986; Colomer, 2001). Since no proposal can beat a Pareto optimal q_r in a single round of voting, no proposal can beat the same q_r in a series of voting. In this sense, there is a one-to-one relationship between the unanimity rule core (i.e., points in equilibrium under unanimity rule) and the Pareto set. Hence, it is easy to see why some scholars might have treated unanimity rule and Pareto optimality almost interchangeably.

Now compare the Pareto optimality predictions to similar predictions for majority rule. Research has demonstrated that unless the distribution of ideal points satisfies radial symmetry (Plott, 1967), the majority rule core will be empty (McKelvey, 1976; Schofield, 1978).[8] In other words, for every alternative there will always be another alternative that a majority prefer to it. This has led several scholars to believe that voting under majority rule may produce just about any outcome in multidimensional space (Riker, 1980). The result has been widely dubbed the "chaos" theorem. In addition to helping us understand claims made about constitutional choice, the results presented in this chapter should help the reader think more carefully about the "chaos" result.

4.3 Pareto Preference

To determine which k-majority rule is most likely to select Pareto preferred alternatives after R rounds of voting, we consider random, sincere, and strategic proposals separately. This helps us determine whether the results require certain behavioral assumptions, such as rationality, or whether they result from the raw properties of the voting rules themselves.

4.3.1 Random Proposals

We start our investigation assuming that proposals are random and voting is sincere.[9] Although we chose to investigate random proposals to study the raw properties of the voting rules themselves, Penn (2009) and Compte and Jehiel (2004) suggest that models with random proposals are fairly realistic for cases where a multiplicity of exogenous actors create proposals. Groseclose and Milyo (2010) further suggest that sincere voting may be common in some deliberative bodies.

To determine which voting rule is most likely to select a Pareto preferred alternative, we first consider a simple comparison of majority rule and unanimity rule using the ideal points in Figure 4.2.[10] Programs for this illustration, and all the simulations presented in the book, are written by the authors in C. In this example, the ideal points are re-scaled to the unit square and the initial status quo, q_1 is fixed at $(0.335, 0.337)$ for both voting rules. We draw a proposal for both voting rules from the unit square and track the outcome of the $1,000$ proposals, each of which represents a different institutional design, under the two voting rules. Each point may

---

[8] If the policy space is single dimensional and ideal points are single peaked and symmetric, then the alternative at the same position as the median voter is in the majority rule core.

[9] An actor votes sincerely if he/she votes for the alternative he/she prefers most among the alternatives available at each stage of the game, without consideration of its effects on the final outcome of the game.

[10] Similar results occur for a single dimension of alternatives.

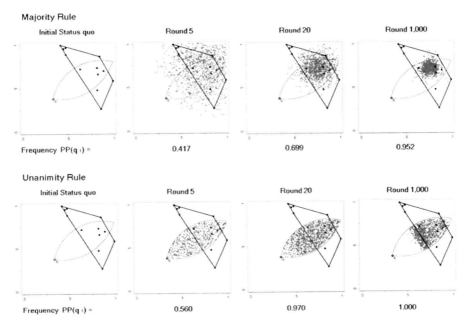

Fig. 4.3 Comparing Majority Rule and Unanimity Rule in Terms of the Pareto Criterion

have potentially different q_r for $r > 1$. Nevertheless, the two voting rules start from the same q_1 and face the same x_r each round.

As Figure 4.3 illustrates, majority rule passes a wide swath of alternatives after five rounds, but tends to concentrate outcomes near the "center" of the Pareto set after 1,000 rounds. Unanimity rule only passes alternatives that are Pareto preferred to q_1, but it often gets stuck at the initial status quo for several rounds, which makes its selection of Pareto preferred alternatives somewhat slow. After 1,000 rounds, all of the outcomes under unanimity rule are in the set of alternatives $PP(q_1)$. A little more than 95% of the cases are in the $PP(q_1)$ set under majority rule. Interestingly, majority rule never selects an outcome Pareto dispreferred to q_1. Moreover, for all of the rounds reported, unanimity rule outperforms majority rule in terms of the Pareto criterion.

This relationship can be generalized in a proposition, which also applies to sincere proposals.

Proposition 2 *Given sincere voting, random (or sincere) proposing, $R \geq 1$, and n-dimensional space. Unanimity rule is at least as likely to select a $PP(q_1)$ outcome as other k-majority rules, where $k < N$.*

Proof. See Dougherty and Edward (2010b) for proof of a similar proposition.

The intuition behind this proposition is simple. Unanimity rule will always select a $PP(q_1)$ alternative if an alternative that can pass is proposed because the $PP(q_1)$

set is identical to the win set[11] under unanimity rule on q_1.[12] Since the win set of q_1 is at least as large for any $k < N$ as it is for $k = N$, k-majority rules with $k < N$ may pass proposals that are not $PP(q_1)$. Figure 4.3 illustrates several of these cases for majority rule.

4.3.2 Strategic Proposals

Dougherty and Edward (2010b) prove a similar proposition for rational proposers, which we extend to k-majority rules in n dimensions without proof.

Proposition 3 *Given that a proposer is one of the voters, the proposer proposes strategically, individuals vote strategically, $R \geq 1$, and information is complete. Unanimity rule is at least as likely to select a $PP(q_1)$ outcome as any k-majority rule, with $k < N$.*

To understand the proof, assume q_1 is Pareto sub-optimal and consider the behavior of a rational proposer in the final round. On the one hand, voting could proceed under unanimity rule. In this case, if q_R was Pareto optimal, then q_R must be Pareto preferred to q_1 because only Pareto preferred alternatives can pass under unanimity rule. Since q_R is Pareto optimal no additional changes can be approved. If q_R was Pareto suboptimal, then the proposer would propose the alternative in the win set of q_1 that is closest to his or her ideal point. This alternative would be Pareto preferred to q_R, and hence pass. Being Pareto preferred to q_R implies it would also be $PP(q_1)$. On the other hand, it is easy to construct examples where groups under other k-majority rules would select outcomes that were not Pareto superior to q_1 under the same circumstances.

Propositions 2 and 3 suggest that unanimity rule is better at producing outcomes that are Pareto preferred to the initial status quo than other k-majority rules. As we shall see, this is not the case for Pareto optimality.

4.4 Pareto Optimality

We now turn to a study of the relationship between various k-majority rules and Pareto optimality. We develop this section at greater length largely because the results are more surprising.

---

[11] The win set is the set of alternatives that can beat the status quo q_r in round r given the voting procedure and sincere voters.

[12] There are only two ways that unanimity rule can fail to attain a $PP(q_1)$ outcome at the end of a game: (1) if q_1 is Pareto optimal (i.e., a Pareto preferred outcome does not exist), and (2) if a Pareto preferred alternative is never proposed.

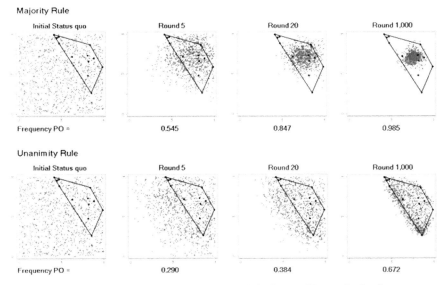

Fig. 4.4 Comparing Majority Rule and Unanimity Rule in Terms of Pareto Optimality

4.4.1 Random Proposals

As in the previous section, we start our investigation assuming that proposals are random and voting is sincere. To illustrate what we might expect in this case, consider another comparison of majority rule and unanimity rule (Figure 4.4). The comparison in this figure differs from the comparison in Figure 4.3 by considering alternatives (i.e., institutional designs) that start in different locations.

In this case, we draw $1,000$ initial status quos from a uniform distribution on the unit square, rather than focusing on a single status quo as in Section 4.3.1. The initial status quos are the same from both majority rule and unanimity rule (see Figure 4.4). We then draw a proposal for each round from a uniform distribution and track the movement of the $1,000$ alternatives under the two voting rules. As the frames in Figure 4.4 illustrate, the alternatives selected under majority rule typically approach the Pareto set fairly quickly. Roughly 80% of the majority rule cases are in the Pareto set after twenty rounds.[13] Unanimity rule takes a longer time to move from its initial point, or any subsequent point, into the Pareto set. After twenty rounds only 38% of the unanimity rule cases are in the Pareto set. As R increases, majority rule's ability to select Pareto optimal results increases as well. For $R = 1,000$, majority

---

[13] Simulations for $N = 5$ on the conditional probability of selecting a Pareto sub-optimal alternative in round r, given that q_r is Pareto optimal suggests that majority rule is increasingly unlikely to move from a Pareto optimal status quo to a Pareto suboptimal outcome as R increases. Similar simulations confirm that majority rule is more likely to move toward Pareto optimal alternatives as R increases.

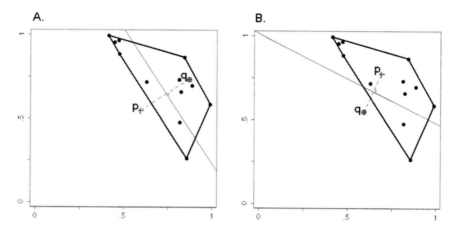

Fig. 4.5 Retention and Attraction

rule selects a Pareto optimal alternative roughly 99% of the time. Unanimity rule selects a Pareto optimal alternative roughly 67% of the time.[14]

To understand why this happens, note that there are two phenomena that affect the outcome — a retentive force and an attractive force. The retentive force, is the ability to stay at a particular point. Unanimity rule is much more capable of retaining Pareto optimal outcomes than majority rule, as demonstrated in Figure 4.5, frame A. This frame depicts two alternatives (q and p), a dotted line connecting q and p, and a thin line, which is the cut line between q and p. For Euclidean preferences (assumed here), a cut line is the right bisector of the line segment between q and p. Cut lines demarcate the space between individuals who prefer the proposal and individuals who prefer the status quo. In frame A, the actors select proposal p in a sincere vote under majority rule (which is Pareto sub-optimal), while they select the status quo q in a sincere vote under unanimity rule (which is Pareto optimal). This suggests that unanimity rule *may* be better at retaining Pareto optimal points than majority rule.

In contrast, the attractive force is the ability to move toward a point. In Figure 4.5, frame B, the choice is between a Pareto sub-optimal status quo q and a Pareto optimal proposal p. If actors vote sincerely, they would chose the Pareto optimal proposal under majority rule and the Pareto suboptimal status quo under unanimity rule. Neither alternative would be Pareto preferred to the other, yet in this case majority rule has produced a Pareto optimal outcome and unanimity rule has not.

Dougherty and Edward (2005, 2010b) show that when these forces are combined, majority rule's advantage in terms of the attractive force generally outweighs its disadvantage in terms of the retentive force. In other words, majority rule is much more likely to bring institutional designs into the Pareto set. Because the majority

---

[14] All of the differences reported in Figure 4.4 are significant at the .01 level.

of ideal points are typically on the same side of the cut line as the Pareto set, groups using majority rule leave the Pareto set less often than one might expect.

We generalize Dougherty and Edward's (2010b) results for random proposals using a number of simulations. For each of the simulations listed below, we study two distributions of the initial status quos, separately: a uniform distribution and a bivariate normal distribution with the mean of dimension j set equal to the median of the ideal points in dimension j.[15] We also study various N from 5 to 99 and R from 1 to 1,000. The simulations are:

1. a uniform distribution of ideal points;
2. ideal points drawn from the population of two-dimensional dw-nominate scores for all U.S. Senators 1789–2008 (this distribution is bivariate in the first dimension and normal in the second dimension, similar to the distribution of Chile's Chamber of Deputies 1998–2000 and the unicameral Congress of Peru 1999–2000).[16]
3. ideal points drawn from the population of two-dimensional w-nominates scores for the European Parliament 1994–2004 (this distribution is multipeaked in both dimensions similar to the National Assembly of the French Fourth Republic 1946–1958 and the Canadian House of Commons 1994–1997);
4. ideal points drawn from the population of two-dimensional w-nominates scores for the Russian Duma 1996–1999 (this distribution is asymmetric in the first dimension similar to the Nicaraguan National Assembly 2000);
5. simulations with uniformly distributed ideal points but "thick" indifference in-difference curves (Ordeshook 1986).[17]

The last case allows for indifference and slightly improves the ability of unanimity rule to select Pareto optimal outcomes with respect to majority rule. For all of the N and R examined in these simulations, majority rule is in most cases at least as likely to select a Pareto optimal outcome as unanimity rule.[18] These differences are statistically significant at the .05 level.

For those who wonder whether we have allowed some kind of hidden decision making costs by limiting unanimity rule to the same number of rounds as majority

---

[15] Proposals are drawn from a uniform distribution in each case.

[16] Different patterns may exist in Chile and Peru for different years.

[17] In this simulation individual i votes for p if and only if $|I_i - p| < |I_i - q| - .025$, and i votes for q if and only if $|I_i - p| > |I_i - q| + .025$. Absolute unanimity rule (which requires *everyone* to vote for the proposal in order for it to pass) performs no better than simple unanimity rule (used here) because absolute unanimity rule implicitly treats "votes to abstain" (indifference in our model) as votes for the status quo. See Dougherty and Edward (2004) for definitions.

[18] There are exceptions. In cases where the distribution of ideal points is extremely skewed, such as 39 ideal points fixed at equal increments between (.01, .75) and (.99, .75) and two ideal points fixed at (.01, .10), and (.99, .10), they find that unanimity rule is slightly more likely to select a Pareto optimal alternative than majority rule if initial status quos and proposals are drawn from a uniform distribution. However, if the first two ideal points are placed at (.01, .75) and (.99, .75), 37 ideal points are placed on a line segment between (.01, y) and (.99, y) exclusive with $y \le .73$, and the final two ideal points are fixed at (.01, .10), and (.99, .10), then majority rule again outperforms unanimity rule.

rule, thereby preventing unanimity rule from having enough time to attain a Pareto optimal outcome, they should note that it takes a large number of rounds for unanimity rule to "catch up" to the rate of Pareto optimal selections under majority rule. For example, if the initial status quo, proposals, and ideal points are all drawn from a uniform distribution, unanimity rule is less likely to produce Pareto optimal results after 1,000 rounds than majority rule is in five rounds. In other words, the differences are not easily rectified by allowing the voting rules to stop at different points.

4.4.2 Sincere Proposals

Although random proposals facilitate a comparison of the raw properties of majority rule and unanimity rule, it may be more useful to study systems with sincere proposals. Individuals may propose sincerely if they solely want to signal constituents (Denzau et al, 1985), procedural rules encourage sincere behavior (Groseclose and Milyo, 2010), or some type of psychological mechanism leads them to propose sincerely such as simple heuristics (Tversky and Kahneman, 1974).

Dougherty and Edward (2010b) present a proposition for sincere proposals which requires the following assumptions:

1. each voter acts as proposer at least once, with one proposer per round;
2. each proposer proposes his/her ideal point; and
3. in each round, voters vote for the alternative closest to their ideal point (i.e., they vote sincerely).

Proposition 4 *Given assumptions 1–3, assume $\kappa < K$. Then a κ-majority rule is at least as likely to select the Pareto optimal alternative in R rounds as a K-majority rule.*

The proof of Proposition 4 is simple. Since only ideal points are proposed, all proposals must be Pareto optimal. Hence the only cases that distinguish the performance of various k-majority rules are the cases where q_1 is Pareto suboptimal. These cases favor k-majority rules with smaller thresholds because for any given q_r the win set of the larger k-majority rule is a subset of the win set of the smaller k-majority rule. Hence, $W_K(q_1) \cap H \subset W_\kappa(q_1) \cap H$, where $W_j(q_1)$ is the k-majority rule win set and H is the convex hull. This logic applies to any number of dimensions.

4.4.3 Strategic Proposals

In seminal works, McKelvey (1976) and Schofield (1978) show that if voting is sincere, information is complete, and the distribution of ideal points does not adhere to radial symmetry, then for any pair (q_1, z) in multidimensional space there exists a finite forward agenda that starts at q_1 and results in z. Given the general absence of equilibria, an agenda setter could make majority rule "wander anywhere" (McKelvey, 1976, p. 480).[19]

Although some have interpreted these results to mean that just about any outcome is possible under majority rule (Riker, 1980), Dougherty and Edward (2010b) show the following result for strategic actors.

Assume (a) a voter is designated proposer in the last round (a variety of proposers and proposal processes can be used in earlier rounds), (b) proposals are strategic in the last round, (c) individuals vote strategically (or sincerely), (d) $R \geq 1$ rounds of voting, and (e) complete information.

Proposition 5 *Fix $k > 0$ and denote by q_R the status quo in round R. Let $W(q_R)$ be the win set of q_R under k-majority rule. Suppose there exists a point $z \in W(q_R)$ of minimal distance to the proposer. Then given assumptions a–e, k-majority rule will select a Pareto optimal outcome in subgame perfect equilibrium (SPE).*[20]

The intuition behind Proposition 5 is that in the final round of voting, a rational proposer will either want to propose the alternative that he/she most prefers that is also in the win set of q_R, or he will prefer q_R and, without loss of generality, propose q_R. Dougherty and Edward use a geometric proof to show that the alternative proposed must be Pareto optimal. Since this argument applies to any status quo in the final round of voting, behavior in earlier rounds is irrelevant to the proof.

The proposition also applies to cases where different k-majority rules are allowed a different number of finite rounds. This is significant because again it helps to address any concern that there are hidden decision making costs in the assumption that all k-majority rules stop after the same number of rounds. If unanimity rule is allowed considerably more rounds than majority rule, both rules will select a Pareto optimal outcome in sub-game perfect equilibrium as long as the number of rounds are finite.

A critical assumption in proposition 5 is that there exists a point in the win set that minimizes the distance from the proposer to the win set. This assumption, which Dougherty and Edward (2010b) refer to as the "attainable minimum assumption," makes an optimal location for the proposal well defined.[21] There are a number of cases where k-majority rules, $k < N$, satisfy the attainable minimum assumption. For example, this assumption is satisfied if the proposer's ideal point is within the win set, q_R is the point on the boundary of the win set that is closest to the proposer, or

---

[19] In their theorems, neither McKelvey nor Schofield model the proposal process nor treat the proposer as someone with specific interests in the outcome of the vote.

[20] See Duggan (2006) for proof of a similar proposition.

[21] This problem is closely related to the open set problem that plagues formal theoretic works, but is often ignored (Krehbiel, 1998; Stewart, 2001). To understand the problem consider a single dimensional spatial voting model with Euclidean preferences and majority rule voting. If $q = 0.3$, the median voter's ideal point is at 0.5, and the proposer's ideal point is at 0.8, then the proposer would like to propose an alternative closest to his/her ideal point that is in the win set of q. Most authors claim this is 0.7. However, since the win set is $(0.3, 0.7)$, i.e. open, it does not include 0.7 and an optimal proposal does not exist.

indifferent individuals vote yes in the final round. Groupthink *may* lead to the latter behavior in the final round (Janis, 1972). Dougherty and Edward (2010b) provide more examples. More importantly, unanimity rule will *always* satisfy the attainable minimum assumption.

Corollary 1 *Given assumptions a–e, unanimity rule will always select a Pareto optimal outcome in subgame perfect equilibrium (SPE).*

If the the attainable minimum assumption does not hold, then the points *on the boundary* of the win set which are closest to the proposer are not technically *in* the win set. In this case, for $k < N$ there will be no equilibrium outcome for and game theory will not make a prediction.

Dougherty and Edward (2010b) argue that if we relax the strict requirements of the game-theoretic framework, then a real world proposer attempting to be rational would propose a point in the win set that is extremely close to the point on the boundary of the win set that is closest to the proposer. The point on the boundary is Pareto optimal, so the proposal will pass and be "very close," almost imperceptibly close, to Pareto optimal. Technically, however, this outcome would not be an equilibrium.

We conclude that among rational actors, unanimity rule is only slightly more adept at selecting Pareto optimal outcomes than other k-majority rules. Furthermore, the outcome under majority rule will be Pareto optimal or very nearly Pareto optimal. This result is *not* an artifact of a structurally induced equilibrium (Shepsle, 1979). It follows simply from rational proposing in a fixed number of rounds.

4.5 Pareto Preferred and Pareto Optimal

Section 4.3 makes it clear that unanimity rule is more effective at producing $PP(q_1)$ results and Section 4.4 makes it clear that majority rule is more effective at producing Pareto optimal results. Interestingly, when both conditions have to be met, unanimity rule is at least as likely as other k-majority rules to select a $PP(q_1)\&PO$ outcome.

4.5.1 Random Proposals

For random proposing and sincere voting, Dougherty and Edward (2010b) use a simulation similar those described in Section 4.4.1 to show that unanimity rule is typically more likely to select a $PP(q_1)\&PO$ alternative than majority rule for $R > 1$. For $R = 1$, unanimity rule and majority rule perform equally because both rules face the same q_1 and x_1. Any x_1 that is Pareto preferred to q_1 will pass under both unanimity rule and majority rule. This is an interesting side note for up or down votes, such as the vote to accept or reject a constitution, but it is a special case.

For $R > 1$, the probability that each voting rule selects a $PP(q_1)\&PO$ outcome typically *decreases* as N increases.[22] Furthermore, unanimity rule typically outperforms majority rule by larger margins as R increases because it increasingly exhausts proposals that are Pareto preferred to q_r, while majority rule may end up selecting outcomes that are not $PP(q_1)\&PO$.

However, there are some important exceptions, one of which is illustrated in Figure 4.3. For the simulation displayed in this figure, majority rule selects a $PP(q_1)\&PO$ alternative with probability 0.270, 0.616, and 0.946 for $R = 5$, 20, 1,000, respectively. Unanimity rule selects a $PP(q_1)\&PO$ alternative with probability 0.252, 0.476, and 0.693 for $R = 5$, 20, 1,000, respectively.

The reason for the exception appears to be the following. For $R > 1$, a necessary condition for majority rule to outperform unanimity rule in terms of $PP(q_1)\&PO$ is for a $PP(q_1)\&\sim PO$ alternative to be proposed before a $PP(q_1)\&PO$ alternative. In this case, unanimity rule may move to a $PP(q_1)\&\sim PO(q_1)$ position x_r which has a smaller set of alternatives Pareto preferred to it than the set of alternatives Pareto preferred to q_1. The initial movement makes a subsequent Pareto improvement less likely and reduces the chances of unanimity rule selecting a $PP(q_1)\&PO$ outcome. Meanwhile, majority rule may move into the $PP(q_1)\&PO$ set quickly because it is not restricted to accepting alternatives that $PP(x_r')$.

It should be noted, however, that the simulation presented in Figure 4.3 is for a status quo that is particularly far from the Pareto set. In Figure 4.4, where there are many status quos at a variety of distances from the Pareto set, unanimity rule is more likely to select a $PP(q_1)\&PO$ alternative than majority rule for each R presented. Moreover, for all the simulations reported in Section 4.4.1, unanimity rule is at least as likely to select a $PP(q_1)\&PO$ outcome as majority rule. Cases where majority rule outperforms unanimity rule are rare.

4.5.2 Sincere Proposals

Recall that in Section 4.4.2, we assume sincere proposing and show that majority rule is more likely to select Pareto optimal outcomes than unanimity. However, if we focus instead on outcomes that are $PO\&PP(q_1)$, then the conclusion is very different.

Proposition 6 *Given assumptions 1–3 (in Section 4.4.2) and $R > 1$, unanimity rule is at least as likely to select a $PP(q_1)\&PO$ alternative as majority rule.*

Proof. See Dougherty and Edward (2010b).

---

[22] There are two reasons why. First, as N increases the Pareto set takes up a larger proportion of the space, making the probability of a drawing a Pareto optimal q_1 increase. Because $PP(q_1)$ requires a Pareto suboptimal q_1, the probability of a Pareto preferred proposal decreases as well. Second, as the Pareto set takes up a larger proportion of the space, the average distance between a suboptimal q_1 and the Pareto set tends to zero. This makes the $PP(q_1)$ set decrease in size as well.

The intuition behind this proposition is that if q_1 is Pareto optimal or the set of points Pareto preferred to q_1 does not contain any ideal points, then majority rule and unanimity rule are equally likely to select a $PP(q_1)\&PO$ outcome. If q_1 is Pareto sub-optimal and the set of points Pareto preferred to q_1 contains at least one ideal point, then unanimity rule has a positive probability of selecting a x_r that is $PP(q_1)\&PO$. The latter is because the status quo remains at q_1 until an ideal point that is $PP(q_1)\&PO$ is proposed and passes. It is fairly easy to generate examples which show that majority rule can have have a zero probability of selecting such a point after the first round.

This proposition extends to a comparison between unanimity rule and other k-majority rules. It also applies to cases where each voter has at least one opportunity to propose, instead of being randomly selected. Hence, if behavior is sincere, unanimity rule should be better at producing $PP(q_1)\&PO$ results than other k-majority rules.

4.5.3 Strategic Proposals

If behavior is strategic, then unanimity is again more capable than majority rule of producing an outcome that is $PP(q_1)\&PO$.

Proposition 7 *Given assumptions a–e (from Section 4.4.3), unanimity rule will select a Pareto optimal outcome that is also Pareto preferred to q_1 in SPE; majority rule may not.*

The proof of the first part of the proposition is a simple extension of the proof of Proposition 5. The proof of the second part can be shown using the example presented in Figure 4.2. Suppose there is one round of voting, q_1 is at the location designated in the figure, and NJ is proposing. It is rational for NJ to propose its ideal point which defeats q_1 by majority rule but not by unanimity rule. Although NJ's ideal point is Pareto optimal, it is not Pareto preferred to q_1.

Obviously, this logic applies to a comparison between unanimity rule and other k-majority rule as well. If constitutional framers want to assure Pareto optimal outcomes that are also Pareto preferred to the initial status quo, then they have good reason to adopt unanimity rule as their voting procedure.

4.6 Experimental Evidence

To test these theoretical results, it would be nice to have data from actual constitutional conventions. However, three major impediments prohibit such a study. First, very few constitutional conventions, or other constitutional processes, have required unanimity rule. This does not imply anything about Buchanan and Tullock's argument because their argument is largely normative. However, it does limit the ability to make comparisons between unanimity rule and other k-majority rules using naturally occurring data. Second, if such data were available, almost all of the variation would be between countries, states, or clubs, etc. Anything correlated with differences between the countries, states, or clubs could result from a spurious relationship. Third, although techniques for estimating ideal points have been available for over a decade (Poole and Rosenthal, 1984; Clinton et al, 2004), scholars are only just now developing techniques to simultaneously estimate the location of ideal points and alternatives (Peress, 2009; Clinton and Meirowitz, 2004). Even those new techniques cannot determine the location of alternatives if a vote is unanimous.

Fortunately, there are other methods of testing the these claims. Dougherty et al (2010) use laboratory experiments. One advantage of laboratory experiments is that they provide a controlled environment where the effect of voting rules, and other treatments, can be isolated. Laboratory experiments also provide an opportunity for researchers to test theories that apply to topics with little or no naturally occurring data, such as voting using unanimity rule.

Dougherty et al (2010) designed their experiment using a paper and paper-and-pencil, no communication format similar to the formats of Fiorina and Plott (1978), McKelvey and Ordeshook (1984), and Bianco et al (2008). They assign subjects to 32 groups of seven subjects each. Each group is assigned a voting rule (either majority rule or unanimity rule) and an information condition (either complete or incomplete). Subjects assigned to a complete information group are given a two-dimensional graph that contains the ideal points of the other subjects as well as their own ideal points and the location of the initial status quo. Subjects assigned to an incomplete information group are given a similar graph without the location of the ideal points of the other subjects. A set of seven ideal points are randomly drawn for each group from a uniform distribution on a 100×100 square, in matched sets. That is, each set of four groups (majority rule, complete; majority rule, incomplete; unanimity rule, complete; unanimity rule, incomplete) are assigned the same set of ideal points so that ideal points matched across treatment conditions.[23] Ideal points are re-drawn in such a way that the initial status quo, $(10, 10)$, was always Pareto sub-optimal.[24]

After the initial practice rounds, subjects are told the initial status quo and asked to propose any (x, y) pair between 0 and 100 inclusive, in increments of 0.01. A subject could propose in future rounds, but only after everyone in the group was given the opportunity to propose first, if they desired. As proposing and voting proceeded, the experimenter records the subject's identification number, their proposal, and the status quo on a chalkboard in the front of the room for all subjects to see. Subject are told the experiment would last exactly ten rounds. After the tenth round, subjects are paid based on the distance between the final outcome and their ideal point, with a maximum of \$15 for an outcome on their ideal point and a minimum of \$1 for an outcome sufficiently far away.

---

[23] As a result, there were only eight sets of ideal points.

[24] None of the sets of ideal points met the condition of radially symmetry needed to make the majority rule core nonempty (Hinich and Munger, 1997).

The results strongly support the arguments presented in this chapter. The few cases where our theoretical results differ from the experimental results all favor majority rule.

At the end of the game, unanimity rule groups were more likely than majority rule groups to select outcomes Pareto preferred to the initial status quo q_1. Seven of the sixteen unanimity rule groups selected Pareto preferred outcomes,[25] while five of the sixteen majority rule groups selected Pareto preferred outcomes. The difference, however, is not statistically significant.

Furthermore, majority rule groups entered the Pareto set more quickly than unanimity rule groups and did a surprisingly good job of staying in the Pareto set. After the first round, majority rule groups were ten times more likely to be in the Pareto set than unanimity rule groups, and they were more than twice as likely to be in the Pareto set in the final round. These differences are statistically significant at the .01 level. More importantly, all of the majority rule groups ended in the Pareto set. Only half of the unanimity rule groups ended there. The reason appears to be that proposers in unanimity rule groups found it difficult to identify proposals that would pass. Among the sixteen unanimity rule groups, six remained at the initial status quo (which was sub-optimal) while two groups moved to a different sub-optimal point and remained at that point for the remainder of the game. Majority rule groups typically entered the Pareto set quickly, and stayed in the Pareto set until the end of the game. Only one of the majority rule groups left the Pareto set during any round of play, only to return to the Pareto set before the game had ended. Surprisingly, the information condition had very little effect on the final results.

Perhaps the most surprising result is that the majority rule and unanimity rule groups were equally likely to select an outcome that was both Pareto preferred to the initial status quo and Pareto optimal. Even though the result is consistent with our theoretical results for sincere proposals, which suggest that unanimity rule is only *at least as likely* to select a $PP(q_1)\&PO$ outcome as majority rule, it contradicts the results for random and strategic proposals which suggest that unanimity rule should strictly outperform majority rule (or at least typically, in the case of random proposals). It is natural to think that unanimity rule should be particularly adept at selecting such points because it only allows a proposal to pass if no one objects. However, the experimental results of Dougherty et al (2010) provide some reason to question this intuition.

---

[25] Five of the unanimity rule groups remained at the initial status quo throughout the game, two moved to a Pareto preferred outcome that was not Pareto optimal, three ended in the Pareto set but not in the set of alternatives Pareto preferred to the initial status quo, and one moved to a outcome that was neither Pareto preferred to the initial status quo nor Pareto optimal. The behavior of the last four groups occurred because at least one subject in each of those groups voted against their preferences, perhaps in a failed attempt to get a more preferred outcome at the end of the game.

4.7 Implications

A fundamental theme of contractarianism is that individuals who are legitimate parties to a social contract must consent to the social contract, either actually or hypothetically. If unanimous agreement is the goal of contractarianism, then it goes without saying that unanimity rule is the best voting rule for assuring unanimity. However, if the goal of contractarians is Pareto efficiency, as argued by many constitutional political economists, and Pareto efficiency is *not* limited to Pareto improvements with respect to the initial status quo, then it is not clear that unanimity rule is the most appropriate voting rule for attaining Pareto efficient results. As we have shown, majority rule is at least as likely to select Pareto optimal outcomes as unanimity rule if proposals are random, sincere, or in some cases strategic.

In contrast, if desirable outcomes should be both Pareto efficient and Pareto preferred to the initial status quo, then unanimity rule typically outperforms majority rule for random, sincere, and strategic proposals. All this suggests that the widely accepted relationship between unanimity rule and Pareto optimality needs to be treated more carefully. Although we leave it to the reader to decide which criterion should be used to judge the most appropriate voting rule for constitutional decision making, we end this chapter with some observations that may help them develop their own opinions.

First, Pareto optimality and Pareto optimality that is Pareto superior to the status quo have one thing in common: Pareto optimality. There are several reasons to value Pareto optimality. One is that failing to produce a set of Pareto optimal institutions means that there is another set of institutions that everyone prefers to it. Besides the obvious normative concerns against Pareto sub-optimal outcomes, such outcomes can invite attempts at additional reform, delegitimize the government, and make it unstable.

Second, Pareto optimality requires that we accept the notion of Pareto preference, but it does not require that we focus exclusively on Pareto preference with respect to the status quo. Whether one wants to add the additional requirement that desirable change should be Pareto preferred to the status quo may hinge on the proper role of the status quo in welfare judgements.

On the one hand, Buchanan and Tullock make a strong case for wanting to protect individual rights and for recognizing that collective decision making can infringe upon those rights unless individuals are restricted to choices that are Pareto improvements. Without that restriction, collective decisions may advantage some individuals to the detriment of others. Resources can be redistributed and a classic tyranny of the majority (or tyranny of the supermajority) can arise. This argument seems particularly compelling in small societies where an initial constitution is being formed.

On the other hand, limiting choices to Pareto improvements from the initial status quo can protect unjust situations that might exist under the status quo (Nozick, 1974, pp. 150–3). For example, if some actors own slaves and emancipating slaves is a core part of a proposed constitution, then requiring all constitutional decisions to be Pareto improvements from the status quo may ultimately result in the preservation

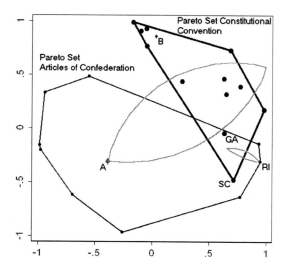

Fig. 4.6 State Positions in the Formation of the Articles of Confederation and the Constitution

of slavery. Such considerations may be particularly important for societies that have a constitution (either written or nonwritten) and want to adopt a new one.

The United States example may shed additional light on the debate. Figure 4.6 displays the now familiar set of ideal points estimated for the Constitutional Convention. It also displays locations estimated for the states during the formation of the Articles of Confederation. The latter was the constitution of the United States prior to the Constitution. According to this figure, states largely changed positions between the two bodies making it likely that the institutional design heading into the convention was Pareto sub-optimal.

Since the Articles of Confederation were formed in Congress voting under a majority of state blocs, the institutions formed in Congress might be in the Pareto set on the left for the Articles of Confederation. Our results for majority rule support such a conjecture. Exactly where the institutional design of the Articles of Confederation, the institutional status quo for the convention, might have been in that set is entirely unknown.

Suppose the institutional design of the Articles of Confederation, was located at the center of the yolk[26] that existed during the period when the Articles were drafted. This is the point marked "A" in the figure (the same location as the status quo in Figure 4.3).

Because the status quo is far from the Pareto set for the Constitutional Convention, a few rounds of majority rule voting at the Constitutional Convention could easily redistribute utility and produce an outcome at, say, B. Such an outcome would

---

[26] In two dimensions, the yolk is the smallest circle that intersects all "median" lines. A median line demarcates the space such that the exact same number of voters on are opposite sides of the median line (McKelvey, 1986; Feld et al, 1988).

be Pareto optimal but not Pareto preferred to the status quo. Moving to such a location might represent a bit of tyranny of the majority because Georgia and South Carolina prefer A and would be made worse off moving from A to B.[27] Requiring Pareto improvements from the status quo avoids this type of tyranny of the majority.

Contrast this with another, more extreme case. If the status quo was at the $1776 - -1777$ position for Rhode Island, marked on the right-hand side of the figure, then the set of alternatives $PP(RI)\&PO$ would be considerably smaller than the set of alternatives $PP(A)\&PO$. Some scholars and constitutional framers might believe that limiting constitutional choices to Pareto improvements from RI might give Rhode Island undue influence over a convention that it never attended. It would certainly prohibit the convention from attaining outcomes near the center of the convention's Pareto set. As Alexander Hamilton wrote:

> If a pertinacious minority can controul the opinion of a majority respecting the best mode of conducting it; the majority in order that something may be done, must conform to the views of the minority; and thus the sense of the smaller number will over-rule that of the greater (Bailyn, 1993, *Federalist* 22, v. 1, p. 511).

In other words, failing to require Pareto improvements to the status quo can lead to tyranny of the majority. But demanding Pareto improvments from the status quo may lead to what Hamilton might describe as a tyranny of the minority.

As it turns out, the actual process used to create the U.S. Constitution was more majoritarian than consensual, though there were moments of consensus in the process. With half of the states in attendance, various clauses in the Constitution passed by a simple majority of attending states. Even the final line of the Constitution, "Done in Convention by the Unanimous Consent of the States present the Seventeenth Day of September …" was passed under majority rule (Farrand 1966, 2: 643–7). Furthermore, Elbridge Gerry, George Mason, and Edmund Randolph refused to sign the Constitution and several other delegates, most notably John Lansing and Robert Yates, opposed the Constitution but left before they could formally vote against it. This left the only remaining delegate from New York, Alexander Hamilton, to sign the Constitution on the behalf of his state when the majority of his delegation was opposed.

Ultimately all the states ratified the Constitution, but even that might not be seen as a evidence of a Pareto improvement from the Articles of Confederation to the Constitution. Riker et al (1996) claims that conventioneers in Rhode Island and New York preferred (1) the Articles of Confederation to (2) the Constitution with Rhode Island and New York included to (3) the Constitution with New York and Rhode Island excluded. If this were the case, then the movement from the Articles of Confederation with all states included (1) to the Constitution with all states included (2) cannot be considered a Pareto improvement regardless of the preferences of the other eleven states. The only reason Rhode Island and New York would have signed, the argument goes, was because nine of the states ratified the Constitution, leaving Rhode Island and New York to choose between inclusion in the new constitution

---

[27] Of course, Figure 4.3 loosely illustrates that in this particular case, majority rule is more likely to produce an outcome in the $PP(A)\&PO$ set than near B.

(2) or not (3). In other words, a super-majority of states removed the option of maintaining the confederation in its full form, and that is what led to a unanimity among states in ratification. Considering the interests of individuals within states only exacerbates the claim that the Constitution was not created by unanimity rule.

If Pareto improvements are somehow necessary for a "fair" change in institutional structure, then we have to live with the notion that the formation of the U.S. Constitution and its institutional structure was probably "unfair." However, if the only requirement is Pareto optimality, with or without Pareto improvement, then the fact that the Constitution was created using more majoritarian procedures may give us reason to withhold such judgement. The procedure used by the Americans may have produced a Pareto optimal result even if it did not produce something Pareto preferred to the status quo.

Chapter 5
Legislative Decision Making

5.1 Introduction

How many individuals must agree before a collective decision is imposed on a community? Buchanan and Tullock (1962) raised that question roughly fifty years ago and answered that it depends on how a community weighs decision costs and external costs. At the constitutional stage decision costs are less consequential. Hence, voting rules that produce Pareto superior and Pareto optimal outcomes (or just Pareto optimal outcomes) should be promoted. The only voting rule that could guarantee such results, and minimize external costs, is unanimity rule. At the legislative stage, the optimal k-majority rule may depend on both external costs and decision costs. With decision costs considered, the sum of decision costs and external costs might be minimized closer to majority rule.

This chapter analyzes the optimal k-majority rule in a context where both external costs and decision costs matter. Since decision costs are almost always important for judging voting procedures in legislatures, we title this chapter "Legislative Decision Making." However, the results presented here should apply to constitutional decision making, or any type of decision making, where the optimal k-majority rule depends on both external costs and decision costs.

As mentioned in Chapter 2, other scholars have considered other types of costs that may be added to the external cost or decision cost functions (Mueller, 1996; Spindler, 1990; Brennan and Hamlin, 2000). These studies have not been fully formalized nor have they carefully examined the effects of functional form on their arguments. Dougherty and Edward (2004) have tried to formalize Buchanan and Tullock's argument in the two-alternative case, but they could not adequately analyze decision costs because decision costs do not vary with k when only the status quo and a single proposal are feasible. Furthermore, the latter work does not extend its analysis to series of votes that are common in legislative settings.

Rather than trying to include new sources of external costs and decision costs, we attempt to assess the claims made by Buchanan and Tullock by creating a framework that can accommodate a series of votes. To conduct our analysis, we formulate a no-

tion of external costs that is analogous to the external costs described by Buchanan
and Tullock and by Mueller (2003). We define a BT-loser as an individual who votes
for a BT-preferred alternative when society chooses against him/her. We then formalize decision costs in a single round as a constant which makes decision costs
in a series largely a function of the probability of passage. This produces several
interesting results.

First, if a society values one cost more than the other, then the mere weight it
puts on decision costs relative to external costs can make $k = 1$ or $k = N$ optimal.
However, even if a society puts no weight on decision costs, it is not always the
case that $k = N$ will be uniquely optimal. Because expected external costs largely
depends on the probability of passing proposals and the probability of passing proposals is logistic-type function of k, there is an almost certain probability of passage
for k near 0 and an almost certain probability of failure for k near N (see Figure 5.1).
As a result, expected external costs can take a logistic-type shape like this as well.
Without decision costs, the flat spots on the right side of the external cost function
can make the optimal k-majority rule a range of k-majority rules near $k = N$ rather
than a singleton.

Second, if external costs and decision costs are equally a concern, then the ho-
mogeniety of the society, as depicted by the preference probabilities introduced in
chapter three, can affect the optima. Everything else equal, if a society is extremely
homogenous with respect to the decisions it has to make, then more inclusive voting
rules might be appropriate. If society is particularly heterogenous with respect to
those decisions, then a less-inclusive voting rule may be appropriate.

Third, the ability to create increasingly desirable proposals between rounds can
affect the optimal k-majority rule. If the political dynamics are such that the probability of passing a proposal quickly increases between rounds, then large k-majority
rules may be preferred. If proposals are not increasingly likely to pass in subsequent
rounds (or their chances improve only slowly), then moderately smaller k-majorities
may be optimal.

Such an analysis can be compared to Mueller's (2003, pp. 76–8) argument that
total costs will be minimized at majority rule because of a "kink" in the decision
cost function. The difference between our results and those claimed by Buchanan
and Tullock, and Mueller, ultimately stems from the fact that for any fixed population, the probability of passage does not decline linearly as k increases. Instead, it
decreases in a logistic-type manner, as shown in Figure 5.1. The difference in shape
has important implications for the external cost function, the decision cost function,
and many of the more intuitive arguments made by Buchanan and Tullock.

5.2 Related Literature

Several authors have tried to determine the optimal k-majority rule. At the legislative
stage, Buchanan and Tullock argue that the optimal k-majority rule should minimize
the sum of external costs and decision costs. Since external costs decrease mono-

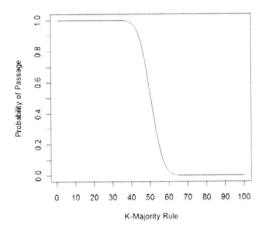

Fig. 5.1 Probability of Passage, $p_1 = p_{-1} = 0.5$, $N = 100$

tonically as a function of k and decision costs increase monotonically as a function of k, they claim the sum is typically minimized in the neighborhood of majority rule. However, there in nothing unique about majority rule within their analysis. In order for majority rule to be the optimum for a wide class of decisions, they thought that there must exist a kink (i.e., a jump discontinuity) in one of the cost functions at $k/N = N/2$. Mueller (2003, p. 77, n.7) take up this issue and writes "*If* constitutional conventions choose parliamentary voting rules by weighting the external and decision-making costs of each rule, as Buchanan and Tullock first posited, *then* there is *no way* to explain the ubiquitous use of the simply majority rule *without* the existence of a discontinuity in one of the two curves at $k/N = N/2$" [emphasis in original].

As noted in Chapter 2, Mueller suggests that the possibility of contradictory decisions for $k/N \leq N/2$ can cause a jump discontinuity in the decision cost function at $N/2$. Hence, decision costs decline by a large jump discontinuity just before majority rule, as shown in Figure 2.2. Combined with a gradually increasing external cost function, such as the one claimed by Buchanan and Tullock, the big jump discontinuity would make majority rule the optimal k-majority rule for a variety of assemblies.

Although a discontinuity such as this suggests that total costs are minimized at majority rule, such a discontinuity may not be necessary for understanding the ubiquitousness of majority rule. This is important because there is no reason to assume that all voting thresholds, less than $N/2$, must produce contradictory outcomes. As long as the rules are well defined there may not be a problem. For example, the U.S. Supreme Court requires only four of its nine judges to issues a writ of certiorari. Once the writ is issued, it is not the case that members opposed to the writ can recall it, even if five members are opposed. The rule allows the status quo of no writ to be replaced with a writ, but it does not allow a writ to be recanted by another coalition of equal or larger size once it has been issued. Put differently, there are cases where small k-majority rules avoid self contradictions. In those cases, Mueller's jump discontinuity does not apply.

More importantly, a big jump discontinuity may not be necessary for guaranteeing that total costs are minimized at or near majority rule. As we will argue later in this chapter, the logistic-type shape of the external cost function implies a sharp drop in the external cost function. Although the exact location of this drop depends on the preference probabilities, many institutional framers may believe that favoring and opposing a proposal is equally likely. In these cases, the external cost function will typically drop in the neighborhood of majority rule. A variety of upward-sloping decision cost functions would then bring constitutional framers to the conclusion that total costs are minimized at or near majority rule.

5.3 One Vote, Two Alternatives

Most of the assumptions used in this chapter are laid out in Chapter 3. Here we also assume that individuals with a strict preference vote sincerely (i.e., for their most preferred alternative in each pair), and indifferent individuals either "vote abstain" or "not vote," without loss of generality.

Buchanan and Tullock (1962, p. 45) described external costs as "the costs that an individual expects to endure as a result of the actions of others over which he has no control." To formalize this idea in a two alternative setting with a proposal and a status quo Dougherty and Edward (2004, p. 171) define the concept of a BT-loser. A BT-loser is an individual who votes against society when society chooses a BT-inferior alternative. That is, an individual who votes for proposal x when x is BT-preferred to the status quo q and society chooses q; or an individual who votes for q when q is BT-preferred to x and society chooses x.[1] A BT loser either suffers a loss because society fails to pass a Pareto preferred proposal that he/she wants or because society passes a proposal that makes some individuals, BT losers, worse off.[2] We can think of the former as a case where a government, or other institution, prevents the adoption of a proposal to which no one would object. That creates a certain amount of external cost due to inaction. We can think of the latter as a case where the actions of a government, or other collective, has adopted a proposal that makes at least some individuals worse than they would be if the action was never taken. Dougherty and Edward (2004) define two types of external costs based on BT losers. "Expected BT-loss" is the expected number of BT losers per person whether or not the proposal passes and "expected BT-loss from a passed measure" is the expected number of BT-losers per person from a passed measure. Buchanan

---

[1] Recall that proposal x is BT preferred to status quo q if and only if it is Pareto preferred to q; otherwise q is BT preferred to x (see Definition 3.5).

[2] In describing external costs, Buchanan and Tullock clearly have in mind the number of individuals who will suffer a cost imposed by others. They do not focus on the intensity of preferences nor try to aggregate intensities across individuals (see their pages 64 and 77–80).

and Tullock seem to presuppose that a proposal passes eventually. In much of our analysis, we do not make this assumption.

Dougherty and Edward (2004) derive the following formulas for these two types of external costs. Expected BT-loss under *absolute* k-majority rule:

$$ec_a = \frac{1}{N} \sum_{s=k}^{N-1} \sum_{t=1}^{N-s} \binom{N}{s}\binom{N-s}{t}(p_1)^s(p_{-1})^t(p_0)^{N-s-t} \cdot t + \sum_{s=1}^{k-1} \binom{N}{s}(p_1)^s(p_0)^{N-s} \cdot s.$$
(5.1)

The factor $1/N$ in front of the sum ensures that we are measuring costs per person. Expected BT-loss under *simple* k-majority rule:

$$ec_s = \frac{1}{N} \sum_{i=0}^{N-1} \sum_{s=\lfloor k-(ik/N)\rfloor+1}^{N-i-1} \binom{N}{i}\binom{N-i}{s}(p_0)^i(p_1)^s(p_{-1})^{N-i-s} \cdot (N-i-s).$$

Let $pass_a$ be the probability that the proposal passes under absolute k-majority rule in the two-alternative case. Expected BT-loss from a passed measure under *absolute* k-majority rule is then:

$$(ec_a|\text{pass}_a) = \frac{1}{N} \frac{\sum_{s=k}^{N-1}\sum_{t=1}^{N-s}\binom{N}{s}\binom{N-s}{t}(p_1)^s(p_{-1})^t(p_0)^{N-s-t} \cdot t}{\sum_{s=k}^{N}\binom{N}{s}(p_1)^s(p_0+p_{-1})^{N-s}}$$

It can also be shown that the probability the proposal passes under *simple k-majority* rule is

$$\text{pass}_s = \sum_{i=0}^{N-1} \sum_{s=\lceil k-(ik/N)\rceil}^{N-i} \binom{N}{i}\binom{N-i}{s}(p_0)^i(p_1)^s(p_{-1})^{N-i-s}.$$

And the Expected BT-loss from a passed measure under *simple k-majority* rule is[3]

$$(ec_s|\text{pass}_s) = ec_s/\text{pass}_s$$
(5.2)

Unless $p_0 = 0$ or $p_1 = 0$, $(ec_a|\text{pass}_a) \neq ec_a/\text{pass}_a$, because of the presence of the second term in equation (5.1). The second term captures BT loss from failure to pass a Pareto preferred proposal. An equivalent term does not exist for simple k-majority rules because simple k-majority rules always pass Pareto preferred proposals.

Figure 5.2 graphs the expected BT-loss from a passed measure for various preference probabilities and $N = 100$. Figure 5.2a presents a case with no indifferent voters and individuals equally likely to favor and disfavor the proposal. As the frame indicates, external costs behave as Buchanan and Tullock described for $k/N > p_1$ — that is, external costs slowly decline as k increases. For k less than p_1 external costs are largely flat, contrary to their descriptions. The expected BT-loss from a passed measure has a similar shape for other preference probabilities. However, as Figures 5.2b and 5.2c indicate, the location of the noticeable decline depends upon the values of p_1 and p_{-1}. If $p_1 > 1/2$, the decline begins at larger values of k. If $p_1 < 1/2$, the decline begins at $k < 50$. This affects the extent to which expected BT-loss from

---

[3] Dougherty and Edward (2004) provide a different, but equivalent, formalization.

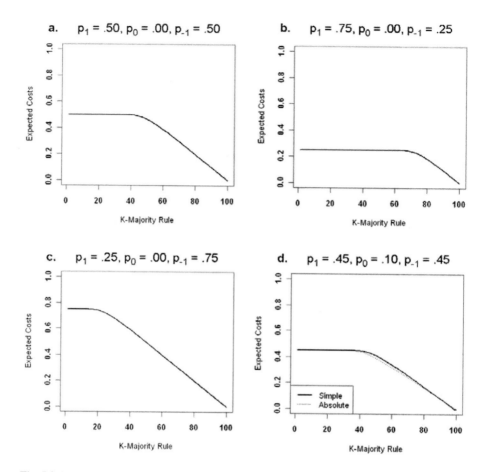

Fig. 5.2 Expected BT-Loss from a Passed Measure, $N = 100$

a passed measure behaves as Buchanan and Tullock might suggest. In Figure 5.2c, the slow decline starts early and most of the figure reflects a gradual decrease as they might claim. However, in Figure 5.2b, the slow decline starts late and external costs are essentially constant for most k, contrary to their claims. Furthermore, the maximum value of the function equals p_{-1}. The reason is that for low k, where the proposal is almost certain to be pass, the expected number of voters saying nay will be $p_{-1}N$, and thus expected external costs should be $p_{-1}N/N$.

Recall that without indifferent voters (or voters who abstain) simple k-majority rule and absolute k-majority rule behave equivalently. Hence, frames a–c depict the expected BT-loss from a passed measure for both simple and absolute k-majority rules. Allowing the possibility of indifferent voters does not change the general shape of the function. It merely separates the simple and absolute cases. In general simple k-majority rule almost always declines to the right of absolute k-majority rule as faintly shown in Figure 5.2d for for $40 < k < 70$.

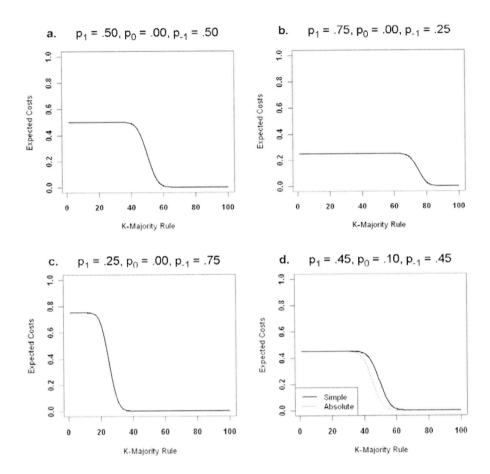

Fig. 5.3 Expected BT-Loss, $N = 100$

Dougherty and Edward (2004) show that these shapes change fairly substantially if it is not presupposed that the proposal passes. Figure 5.3 graphs the expected BT-loss for the same preference probabilities as shown in Figure 5.2. The only difference is that we do not presuppose that the proposal passes. This gives the external cost function more of a logistic-type shape. For large populations, such as $N = 100$, almost all of the decrease in expected BT-loss takes place in a narrow interval centered around $k/N = p_1$. If p_1 is small (as in Figure 5.3c), then the drop starts at smaller values of k. If p_1 is large (as in Figure 5.3b), then the drop starts at large values of k. As in the previous figure, the height of the expected loss function is fully determined by p_{-1}.

Keep in mind that the probability of failing to pass a Pareto preferred proposal is a rare occurrence and it cannot occur if $p_0 = 0$. Hence, the marked difference in shapes between Figure 5.3 and Figure 5.2 is not typically due to the new type of BT loser. Instead it results from the conditional expectation of presupposing that the measure passes. For simple k-majority rules this is operationalized by the inclusion of the probability of passage in the denominator of equation (5.2). With the denominator, we get shapes like Figure 5.2a. Without the denominator, we get shapes like Figure 5.3a. Dividing by the probability of passage is fully responsible for the more gradual decline in the earlier figure.

With indifferent voters absolute and simple k-majority rules do not select equivalently. Instead, simple k-majority rule dips to the right of absolute k-majority rule, as depicted in Figure 5.3d. This is because for any k, simple k-majority rule is more likely to pass a proposal than absolute k-majority rule, with noticeable differences for values of k/N near p_1.

At this point it would be interesting to include some formalization of decision costs. Decision costs are the "time and effort ... required to secure agreement" (Buchanan and Tullock, 1962, p. 68). Buchanan and Tullock argue that decision costs increase with k because larger k-majority rules make it more difficult to formulate *successful* proposals. This is not the case in a two-alternative framework, with a proposal and a status quo. A single proposal prohibits any restructuring of a measure to make it more palatable. Hence, the time and effort required to consider a single proposal would be the same for all k. Decision costs would be constant. In order to allow decision costs to vary with k, we have to consider multiple alternatives in a series.

5.4 A Series of Votes, Multiple Alternatives

We now extend the analysis to include multiple alternatives in a series of votes. For this part of the analysis assume that an assembly meets to pass a resolution on some issue and that voters are uncertain about the preferences of other voters. A first proposal is made, and if the proposal were put to vote, individuals would vote for or against the proposal with probabilities $p_{1,1}$ and $p_{-1,1}$ respectively. Here $p_{-1,1}$ indicates the probability of opposing the proposal in round 1. For $r > 1$, $p_{1,r}$ (resp. $p_{-1,r}$) is the probability that an individual favors (resp. opposes) the proposal in round r given that the proposals in the previous rounds have been defeated. For simplicity, we assume that there are no indifferent voters. In other words, $p_{0,r} = 0$. Hence, the distinction between simple and absolute is no longer important and the only BT loss comes from a passed proposal. We also assume:

    (i) in each round, the probabilities $p_{1,r}$, $p_{-1,r}$ are the same for all individuals; and

    (ii) in each round, a voter's preference is independent of the preferences of the other voters.

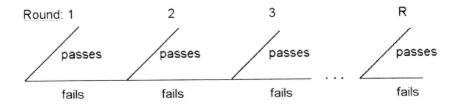

Fig. 5.4 A Finite Series of Votes

After the motions is proposed, it is discussed then put forward for a vote. If the motion passes, the process ends. If the motion is defeated, then a new proposal is made with new values for $p_{1,r+1}$ and $p_{-1,r+1}$. To model the notion of continuously improving proposals, we assume that the information gathered in the discussions of the previous proposal and the subsequent vote are enough to make the the new motion more likely to pass than the motion in the previous round (i.e., $p_{1,r} > p_{1,r-1}$). The procedure is then repeated. In each round a proposal is discussed, followed by either passage of the proposal or a new proposal. In a finite series, successive proposals are made until a proposal passes or the final round R is reached.

The process follows a "successive" voting procedure (Rasch, 2000). That is, the initial status quo q_1 is paired against a proposal x_1 in round 1. If x_1 passes, voting ends. If x_1 fails, q_1 is paired against x_2 in round 2, and so on, for a total of R rounds (see Figure 5.4). In a successive procedure, voting continues until a proposal passes or the final round R is reached where the proposal can either pass or fail. The successive procedure is widely used by national legislatures in Europe, including the national legislature in France, Germany, Spain, Greece, and Norway, to name a few (Rasch, 2000). A different procedure, often referred to as an amendment procedure (or elimination procedure) is used in the United States, Canada, and Great Britain.[4] The successive procedure need not be limited to legislative decision making. It may also apply to constitutional decision making in small communities and to other types of decisions.

5.4.1 Decision Costs

To formalize decision costs in this setting, we assume that each round of proposal/discussion imposes the same decision making costs on the assembly, $c > 0$.

We also assume that p_1 increases in each round by an increment, that increment is either α or α/r, where $\alpha > 0$ is some constant. Since $p_1 + p_{-1} = 1$, this means p_{-1} will decrease by the same increment. Assuming α creates a constant increase in the probability of favoring a proposal between rounds. Assuming α/r implies that as

---

[4] The procedure described in Chapter 4 should be considered a third type. Agendas move backward in the amendment procedure and forward in Chapter 4.

r increases the probability of finding a favorable proposal increases at a decreasing rate.[5]

5.4.2 External Costs

To formalize our notion of external costs, let $E[C_r]$ denote the expected BT loss from round r, and F_r denote the event "the proposal is defeated in round r." By the properties of conditional expectation, we have for $r > 1$

$$E[C_r] = E[C_r|F_1 \cap \ldots \cap F_{r-1}]P[F_1 \cap \ldots \cap F_{r-1}]$$
$$= E[C_r|F_1 \cap \ldots \cap F_{r-1}]P[F_1]P[F_2|F_1]\ldots P[F_{r-1}|F_1 \cap \ldots \cap F_{r-2}].$$

Under the assumptions described in Section 5.4,

$$P[F_1] = \sum_{s=0}^{k-1} \binom{N}{s}(p_{1,1})^s(p_{-1,1})^{N-s},$$

and for $1 < j \leq R$,

$$P[F_j|F_1 \cap \ldots F_{j-1}] = \sum_{s=0}^{k-1} \binom{N}{s}(p_{1,j})^s(p_{-1,j})^{N-s};$$

and

$$E[C_r|F_1 \cap \ldots \cap F_{r-1}] = \sum_{s=k}^{N}(N-s) \cdot \binom{N}{s}(p_{1,r})^s(p_{-1,r})^{N-s}.$$

Finally, we define external costs in a series as

---

[5] We have chosen to formalize decision costs as constant across rounds and let the differences between various k depend on the probability of passage. There are certain advantages to such a formalization. First, it is simple. Second, it captures Buchanan and Tullock's notion that decision costs are smaller in more homogenous populations (Buchanan and Tullock, 1962, pp. 115–6), where $p_{1,1}$ should be greater, than in more heterogeneous populations. Third, the formalization is consistent with Buchanan and Tullock's claim that decision costs among k members of a group size N will generally be smaller than unanimity among a group of size k (Buchanan and Tullock, 1962, pp. 106–8). For example, in a series of votes decision costs should be smaller for a voting threshold of 51 members out of a group of 100 than for a voting threshold of 51 members out of 51. This is because there are more combinations of a coalition of 51 members out of 100 than there are combinations of 51 members out of 51 (Buchanan and Tullock, 1962, pp. 106–8). Fourth, because of the associative property of addition and multiplication, c also provides a relative weight between decision costs and external costs in the total cost function. However, there are disadvantages to such a formalization. First, the exact value of c might not be easy to determine. Everything else equal, larger values of c may cause total costs to be minimized at smaller values of k. Second, our formalization of decision costs does not model bargaining and other game-theoretic processes explicitly. It only "assumes" that there is a process that increases the probability of passage each round.

$$EC = \sum_{r=1}^{R} E[C_r].$$

In the last equation R could be infinite, which implies that a proposal is never accepted.

5.5 Results

Figure 5.5 presents decision costs (thick lines), external costs (thin lines), and total costs (dashed lines) for the initial preference probabilities $p_{1,1} = p_{-1,1} = 0.5$ and $c = .01$. Each frame varies by the increment used to increase $p_{1,1}$ and decrease $p_{-1,1}$ between rounds. In frames a and b, $p_{1,1}$ is increased by a constant. We continue the series until $p_{1,r} = 1.0$. For $\alpha = 0.1$, this implies that the series will last at most six rounds. For $\alpha = 0.001$, the series lasts at most 501 rounds. Hence, a proposal will pass at the end of both sequences.

If a proposal will always pass, why aren't the external costs the same for every k-majority rule? The answer is that smaller k-majority rules will be more likely to pass the proposal early, when $p_{1,r}$ is smaller, $p_{-1,r}$ is larger, and the external external costs associated with $p_{-1,r}$ are high. Larger k-majority rules are more cautious. They are unlikely to pass a proposal until $p_{1,r} > k/N$. In those cases, $p_{1,r}$ is larger, $p_{-1,r}$ is smaller, and external costs associated with $p_{-1,r}$ are small as well. The differences are not in whether the proposal passes by the end of the series. In these two series they certainly will. The differences are whether a k-majority rule will allow a proposal to pass in an early round or will cause the assembly to wait until later rounds when proposals will appeal to a large portion of the population.

Consider frame a. In this case, the probability of favoring the proposal increases quite rapidly between rounds. External costs in this frame look surprisingly similar to the expected BT loss from a passed measure for the two-alternative case (Figure 5.2a). However, unlike the one-shot case, all $k > 92$ produce roughly zero external costs. In addition, decision costs start near .01, for all $k < 45$, because proposals are easily passed for such k. After that point decision costs increase linearly for $45 \leq k \leq 100$. The increase is slow because $p_{1,r}$ increases rapidly to 1 as r increases. This rapid increase means that for larger k, $p_{1,r}$ quickly exceeds k/N, which prevents larger k-majority rules from incurring much decision costs. Because external costs are much larger than decision costs for almost every k, the sum of the two functions is minimized at $k = 99$ and 100. Such a result supports the notion that unanimity rule or a near unanimity rule are ideal (Wicksell, [1896] 1967).

Frame b differs from frame a by the rate at which the probability of favoring the proposal increases between rounds and the total number of rounds before $p_{1,r}$ converges to 1. In this case, external costs look fairly similar to those frame a. The major difference between the two frames is the decision costs. Decision costs start at the same location as in frame a, but make a sharp increase shortly after .5. This steep incline is due to the fact that $p_{1,r}$ increases very slowly to 1. The slow increase

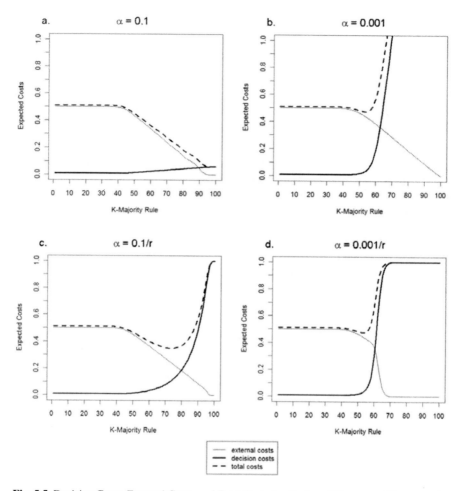

Fig. 5.5 Decision Costs, External Costs, and Total Costs in a Series of Votes, $c = .01$

Note: $p_{1,1} = p_{-1,1} = 0.5$.

implies that for $k > 50$ there will be many rounds where $p_{1,r} < k/N$. These are cases where the proposal is very unlikely to pass. Combined with external costs such decision costs creates a unique minimum in the total cost function at $k = 52$. This results supports the notion that majority rule or a near majority rule should be chosen.

Frames c and d depict results for increasing $p_{1,r}$ at a marginally decreasing rate. In these cases, $p_{1,r}$ reaches 1.0 only for extremely large R. Hence, we stop the series after $R = 100$ rounds.[6] The meaningful difference between the result displayed in frames c and d is the rate at which the probability of favoring proposals increases, particularly in earlier rounds.

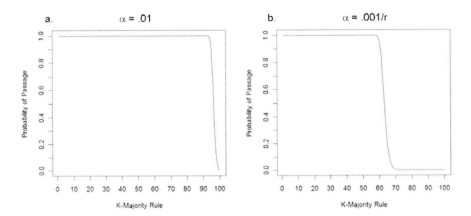

Fig. 5.6 The Probability of Passing a Proposal in 100 Rounds or Less

Note: $p_{1,1} = p_{-1,1} = 0.5$.

Frame c shows the results for a slowly increasing α. Again, external costs slowly decline after $k = 45$ similar to the previous frames. Even though $p_{1,100} < 1$, the probability of passing a proposal in 100 rounds or less is roughly 1 for almost all values of k (see Figure 5.6a) — hence the almost linear decline in external costs. At the same time, decision costs increase more abruptly than in frame a but less abruptly than in frame b, because $p_{1,r}$ increases slower in frame c than in frame a and more quickly than in frame b. Combined, the total cost function is minimized at $k = 74$. In this case, a supermajority rule, such as $3/4$ths rule might be recommended for the community.

Finally, frame d displays a case that is identical to the one depicted in frame c except the rate that $p_{1,r}$ increases much slower. After $r = 100$, the cumulative probability of passing a proposal is much smaller for larger values of k as shown in Figure 5.6b. The difference in the cumulative probability of passage produces two noticeable effects. First, the external cost function looks much more like a logistic-type function, as in the two alternative case without a presupposition that the proposal passes (Figure 5.3a). The reason for this is that a proposal is not likely to pass for $k > p_{1,1}N$. In Figure 5.6a, a proposal is likely to pass under such k and external costs decline more gradually as a result. Second, the decision cost function in frame d increases sharply, as in frame b or c, but it takes on a more logistic-type shape.

---

[6] For $\alpha = 0.1/r$, $p_{1,r}$ converges to 1 at $r = 226$. For $\alpha = 0.001/r$, $p_{1,r}$ converges to 1 at $r > 100,000$.

Despite these differences the total cost functions in frames *b* and *d* are fairly similar. In this case, the optimum is $k = 53$, similar location to frame *b*.

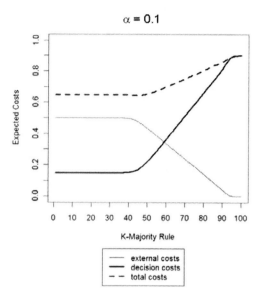

Fig. 5.7 Decision Costs, External Costs, and Total Costs in a Series of Votes, $c = .15$

Note: $p_1 = p_{-1} = 0.5$.

Of course, different values for decision costs per round, c, will effect total costs. Figure 5.7 presents results for $c = .15$. Otherwise, the parameters are identical to those depicted in Figure 5.5a. Note that in this case, total costs are more or less constant for all $k < 52$, making a wide range of less-inclusive k-majority rules optimal. There are two reasons. First, for large k, decision costs dominate external costs in this case, and second, for $k > 45$, decision costs have a moderately steep slope compared to Figure 5.5a. In general, larger c will imply that the optimum is a less-inclusive voting rules as one might otherwise expect.

Altering the initial preference probabilities, $p_{1,1}$ and $p_{-1,1}$, also has an effect similar to the two-alternative case. If $p_{1,1} = 0.7$ and $p_{-1,1} = 0.3$ (not shown), external costs have an initial value of .3 and decline slowly for values of k such that $k \geq 70$ (similar to Figure 5.2b). If decision costs increase abruptly, as they do for $\alpha = .001$ and $\alpha = .001/r$, then the steep increase will begin at values of k near $k = p_{1,1}(N) = 70$. In these cases, supermajority rules near 75 might be optimal. If decision costs increase slowly as a function of k, as they do for $\alpha = .1$, then the optimal k-majority rule will be a small range near unanimity.

In contrast, if $p_{1,1} = 0.3$ and $p_{-1,1} = 0.7$, external costs will start at .7 and decline slowly for values of k such that $k \geq 30$ (similar to Figure 5.2c). For sharply increasing decision costs, such as those from $\alpha = .001$ and $\alpha = .001/r$, the optimal k-majority rule would be in the vicinity of $k = 35$. Hence, one implication is that if a society is extremely homogenous from the beginning, it might want to consider a more inclusive k-majority rule. If a society is particularly heterogenous, it might consider a less inclusive k-majority rule.

5.6 Conclusion

Any formalization of decision costs and external costs should include the likelihood of passing proposals. After all, the probability of passing a proposal affects the time and effort needed to reach an agreement and the ability to impose costs on other individuals. In our model, the probability of passage is is not linear across k. Instead, it is a logistic-type function as depicted in Figure 5.1. For any given $(p_{1,r}, p_{-1,r})$ there are k where the proposal will almost certainly pass and and other k where it will almost never pass. As a consequence, there are often horizontal regions in decision costs and external costs functions near the extremes. These horizontal regions provide some of our most interesting, but perhaps most unintuitive, results. For example, unanimity rule may guarantee zero external costs, but that does not mean it should be treated as uniquely minimizing external costs. For all practical purposes, other k-majority rules near unanimity may be equally adept at minimizing external costs in some circumstances. Hence, if we cared solely about external costs we might get a range of optimal voting rules. In this sense, unanimity rule might be an ideal voting rule for the constitutional phase of decision making. However, even without decision costs, it would not be a unique ideal.

In the same vein, $k = 1$ may not be uniquely qualified for minimizing decision costs. A range of k-majority rules may produce roughly the same decision costs as $k = 1$.

In a series of votes, the optimal k-majority rule depends on several factors, one of which is the probability of passage, just described. Another is the ability to create increasingly desirable proposals between rounds. Suppose an institutional framer assumes that favoring and opposing proposals is equally likely. Under such conditions, larger k-majority rules, such as unanimity rule, should be considered if individuals can reformulate proposals in a way that substantially increases the probability of favoring measures between rounds. If the probability of favoring proposals increases quickly, larger k-majority rules will inhibit proposals that hurt minorities without amassing large decision costs. However, if proposals can only be reformulated in a way that slowly increases the probability of favoring a proposal between rounds, then institutional framers might have reason to favor k-majorities near $p_{1,1}(N)$. The slow increase in the probability of favoring a proposal would imply significantly larger decision costs for $k > (.5)N$. If favorable proposals evolve moderately, between the two extremes, then institutional framers may want to adopt supermajority rules, such as 3/4ths rule.

Another factor that affects the optimal k-majority rule is the decision costs per round, c. This variable serves at least two purposes in our formulation: it helps to put decision costs and external costs on a common scale and it provides a relative weighting between the two terms in the total cost function. As should be obvious, for each set of parameters, there will always be a sufficiently large value of c that will make $k = 1$ optimal (perhaps among other k-majority rules in the neighborhood of $k = 1$) and a sufficiently small value of c that will make $k = N$ optimal (perhaps among other k-majority rules in the neighborhood of $k = N$).

Furthermore, the optimal k-majority rule seems to depend on the homogeneity of the society, as depicted by the initial preference probabilities ($p_{1,1}$, $p_{-1,1}$). If a society is extremely homogenous from the beginning so that, say, $p_{1,1} = .7$, then it might want to consider a more inclusive k-majority rule. If a society is particularly heterogenous, especially with respect to the decisions that have to be made, then it might want to consider a less inclusive k-majority rule (similar to our results for $p_{1,1} = .3$). External costs will be greater in the latter case, but these costs will decline quickly and they will be offset by increasing decision costs that can mount up as individuals disagree.

Contrast this result with a claim made by Buchanan and Tullock (1962, p. 115).

The implication of this hypothesis suggests that the more homogenous community should adopt more inclusive rules for the making of collective decisions. However, the homogeneity characteristic affects external costs as well as decision-making costs. Thus, the community of homogenous persons is more likely to accept less restrictive rules even though it can "afford" more restrictive ones. By contrast, the community that includes sharp differences among individual citizens and groups cannot afford the decision-making costs involved in near unanimity rules for collective choice, but the very real fears of destruction of life and property from collective action will prompt the individual to refuse anything other than such rules.

Buchanan and Tullock seem to talk themselves out of a conclusion similar to ours. They suggest that more inclusive rules, like unanimity rule, might be more appropriate for both homogenous and heterogenous societies. Our results suggest that their initial intuition may have been more accurate. Everything else equal, larger k-majority rules will be optimal in homogenous societies and smaller k-majority rules will be optimal in heterogenous societies.

Finally, this analysis may provide a loose explanation for the ubiquitous use of majority rule in legislative settings. If an institutional framer is uncertain about whether individuals will typically get along and favor each other's proposals or conflict with their colleagues and oppose each other's proposals, he/she may assume that favoring and opposing proposals is equally likely, in which case, the optimal k-majority rule might be near majority rule, particularly if he/she believes a series of votes might be long and protracted. This seems to be the case in many legislative settings where policies on defense, transportation, and public welfare seem to be stepping stones in a continuous progression of decision making. With a sharply increasing decision cost function, total costs may be minimized at or near majority rule. This provides a partial justification for the wide use of majority rule without requiring a big jump discontinuity in the decision cost function.

Chapter 6
Electoral Decision Making

6.1 Introduction

Everyone remembers the 2000 U.S. presidential election between George W. Bush and Al Gore. Bush won more Electoral College votes than Gore, and with it the presidency. Nevertheless, Gore won more popular votes than Bush. Many argued that Gore should have been elected the president because he won the plurality of the popular vote. Making such an argument implies that one voting rule (plurality rule) is more desirable than another voting rule (the Electoral College) and opens up a discussion about the desirable properties of voting rules and which voting rule is best. Although one voting rule may be particularly adept at fulfilling one criterion, other voting rules may be particularly adept at fulfilling other criteria. Since no voting rule satisfies a small subset of reasonable criteria (Arrow, 1951), the natural question is which rules are most likely to satisfy common norms?

To answer that question, constitutional framers may have to consider a new set of criteria that differ from those applied to legislatures. Legislative decisions and electoral decisions are rarely conducted the same way due to the nature of the decision. Legislative decisions are usually made by a small to medium body of professionals who repeatedly deliberate and vote on a single issue. Electoral decisions are usually made by the citizens at large who cannot be expected to meet and vote on the same issue too often. Moreover, legislative decisions are usually made by comparing alternatives pairwise under some k-majority rule. This allows legislatures (and executives) to compare different versions of a bill in head-to-head competitions. Maintaining the status quo is always an option. Electoral decisions often require voters to choose among three or more alternatives simultaneously without special consideration for the status quo. This means the voting rule has to remain neutral with respect to the candidates. In contrast, all the k-majority rules examined in the previous chapter favor the status quo in at least one case and violate neutrality.[1]

---

[1] Simple majority rule violates neutrality by selecting the status quo if #*yeas* = #*nays* (see Definition 3.2). In May's (1952) theorem, majority rule does not violate neutrality because May assumes majority rule ties if #*yeas* = #*nays*. Our version is more commonly used in practice (Rasch, 1995).

If a k-majority rule, such as majority rule, is applied to an election, the voting rule needs to be modified to determine which candidate will win the election if a majority is not attained. Voting rules used in legislatures do not require such modifications. If all legislators voice a strict preferences and the status quo is specified, one of the two alternatives will win a k-majority in any *pairwise* comparison.

In this chapter, we examine voting rules used to elect representatives in single-member districts, that is, voting rules that select one person to represent that district, which is common in Great Britain and some of its former colonies such as India and the United States. In the vernacular, we examine a narrow class of collective choice rules. Specifically, we examine voting rules that produce a single best element (or winner). Although we envision the study as one where a single candidate is elected to public office, the analysis might be of interest to scholars who want to select a Pareto optimal policy out of a list of Pareto optimal policies. We do not attempt to analyze rankings of social preferences, which would be useful for studies of proportional representation, though at least one of the voting rules we examine produces a social preference order. The properties of multi-member districts are worthy of further investigation.

To narrow our study, we examine four voting rules: (1) plurality rule, (2) majority rule with a runoff, (3) instant runoff voting, and (4) Borda count. The first three are the most commonly used voting rules in national elections with single-member districts. The fourth has received considerable attention in the social choice literature. We compare these voting rules in terms of the probability that they adhere to six criteria (analyzed separately): the (1) Condorcet winner criterion, (2) the Condorcet loser criterion, (3) the majority criterion, (4) consistency, (5) reversal symmetry, and (6) independence of eliminated alternatives. All of these criteria have been used by previous scholars (Mueller, 2003).

To compare the performance of our voting rules with respect to each other, we simulate electoral voting using a single-dimensional spatial voting model. This allows us to determine the probability that each voting rule adheres to a criterion in a context that has been widely accepted in the literature. We find that the Borda count performs at least as well as the other three voting rules on all of the criteria, except the majority criterion and in some cases of the Condorcet winner criterion. However, if we drop the assumption that both the voters and the candidates are drawn from a normal distribution, then the Borda count *can* perform the worst on the Condorcet winner criterion. The latter is particularly interesting, because earlier research suggests that Borda count is more likely to select a Condorcet winner than common voting rules for specific preference distributions. We also find that plurality rule, majority rule with a runoff, and instant runoff voting outperform Borda count in terms of the majority criterion. And among those three procedures, majority rule with a runoff performs at least as well as the other two on the remaining criteria. Plurality rule tends to underperform on all of the criteria despite the fact that it is the most widely used voting rule in single-member districts (Farrell, 2001).

6.2 Probabilistic Comparisons

There are several ways to approach the problem of determining which voting rule is "best." First, we might define a set of axiomatic properties and determine which voting rules adhere to those properties. For example, May (1952) suggested that a desirable voting rule should adhere to four criteria. He required that a voting rule be decisive (i.e., it must pick a winner), adhere to anonymity (i.e., treat each voter identically), maintain neutrality (i.e., treat each alternative equally), and adhere to positive responsiveness (i.e., if society prefers x at least as much as y and one individual changes his vote from y to x or from y to indifference while all other votes remain unchanged, then society should society should strictly prefer x to y). May showed that in two alternative choices with all eligible citizens voting, a majority rule that ties if #*yeas* = #*nays* is the only voting rule that satisfies these four conditions.[2] Furthermore, these four conditions imply his type of majority rule. Of course, the theorem does not apply to elections with three or more candidates because majority rule may not be decisive in those cases.

More importantly, most axiomatic theorems show that without making interpersonal comparisons of utility, *no* voting rule can adhere to a small set of axioms (Roberts, 1980; Fishburn, 1987). This is the nature of Arrow's (1951) well-known impossibility theorem. Arrow showed that no social welfare function can adhere to four conditions without producing a dictatorship. These conditions were an unrestricted domain (i.e., all possible individual preference rankings must be permitted), independence of irrelevant alternatives (i.e., for any pair of alternatives x and y, the changes in individual preferences for other alternatives such as w and z should have no impact on the social ranking of x and y), transitivity, and the weak Pareto criterion (Definition 3.4). This includes voting rules previously used and voting rules not yet created.

Perhaps one limitation of the standard, axiomatic approach is that it leads to all-or-nothing conclusions. Either a voting rule adheres to a set of criteria over an unrestricted domain or it does not. In May's theorem only one voting rule adheres to the criterion. In Arrow's theorem, none do.

Since no voting system satisfies all the objectives that an institutional designer may have in mind, it may be useful to relax the condition of an unrestricted domain and ask which systems are *more likely* to satisfy a desirable set of objectives in a common domain. In other words, we might ask ourselves whether these paradoxes are the result of a few concocted examples or whether they constitute likely problems. To do this, we would determine the probability that each voting rule adheres to a criterion or set of criteria rather than requiring that it always does or never does. This approach has received slightly less attention in the social choice literature,[3] even though it can be a powerful tool for comparing voting rules that violate a cri-

---

[2] May's majority rule is similar to simple majority rule, except everyone votes and if #*yeas* = #*nays* the tie is resolved with a flip of a coin. See Laruelle and Valenciano (2010) and Freixas and Zwicker (2009) for extensions of May's theorem to cases with quorum requirements and nonvoters.

[3] Studies of the probability of satisfying various voting criteria include Merrill (1984), Lepelley (1993), Lepelley et al (2000), Gehrlein (2002b), and Dougherty and Edward (2010a)

terion, or set of criteria, for one or more sets of preference orders. The approach also helps to determine whether a voting rule that violates a criterion violates it so rarely that it should be treated as similar to a voting rule that never does. Keep in mind that examining the probability of adhering to a criterion differs from the study of probabilistic voting rules (Intriligator, 1973; Coughlin, 1992). Those studies investigate voting rules that chose candidates probabilistically. In our case, all voting rules chose deterministically. We simply ask how likely a voting rule will adhere to a particular criterion, and we do this for each criterion separately.

6.2.1 Voting Rules

At the national level, more people are represented by an elected official presiding over a single-member district than under any other voting system in the world (Farrell, 2001). A single-member district is one where a predetermined constituency, such as those residing within a geographic area, elect a single person to represent them in political office. The three most prevalent voting rules for electing such officials at the national level are plurality rule, majority rule with a runoff, and instant runoff voting. Using the term "voters" to refer to citizens who turn out and vote, these rules are defined as follows.

Definition 6.1. *Plurality rule*: The candidate who is ranked first by the largest number of voters wins the election.

Plurality rule (also known as "first past the post") is used in national elections in Canada, India, Iran, Mexico, South Korea, Thailand, the United Kingdom, the United States, and Yemen to name a few. More people in the world elect members to a national public office under plurality than under any other system — thanks in large part to India's large population (Farrell, 2001).

Definition 6.2. *Majority rule with a runoff (MRR)*: If one candidate receives more than half of the first place votes cast, he/she wins the election. Otherwise, a second election is held between the two candidates receiving the most first place votes. The candidate receiving the most votes on the second ballot wins the election.

MRR has French origins. It is used for legislative elections in France, for presidential elections in Austria, Bulgaria, Chile, France, Madagascar, Portugal, Russia, and Ukraine, to name a few. It is also used in U.S. local elections in Georgia, Louisiana, and parts of Florida.

Definition 6.3. *Instant runoff voting (IRV)*: Each voter ranks the candidates in order of his/her preference. If one candidate receives more than half of the first place votes cast, he/she wins. Otherwise, the candidate(s) with the fewest first place votes is eliminated and voter ballots for that candidate(s) are redistributed to the next highest candidate in each voter's preference order. The process is repeated until one candidate obtains a majority of first place votes among the remaining candidates.

IRV is used to elect members of the Australian House of Representatives, the national parliament of Papua New Guinea, some mayors in New Zealand, the president of Ireland, and in Burlington, VT, San Fransisco, CA, and Santa Fe, NM. It is also used to select the President of the American Political Science Association. IRV is a type of single transferable vote scheme applied to single-member districts.

The next voting rule has been rarely used in national elections, but it has received considerable attention in the social choice literature because it captures information about each individual's complete ranking of the candidates (Van Newenhizen, 1992; Heckelman, 2003; Saari, 2008). Let m be the number of candidates in an election.

Definition 6.4. *Borda count*: Each voter ranks the candidates in order of his/her preference. An election official gives each candidate a score between 1 and m based on the voter's ranking of the m candidates. Specifically the candidate ranked first receives m points, the candidate ranked second receives $m - 1$ points, ..., the candidate ranked last receives 1 point. The candidate who receives the greatest sum of these points wins the election.

The Borda count is used in Slovenia to elect the member of its National Assembly who represents ethnic Italians and the member who represents ethnic Hungarians. It is also used to nominate presidential candidates in Kiribati (Reilly, 2002), to determine the Most Valuable Player in Major League Baseball, and to nominate the Heisman Trophy winner. A variation of the rule is used to elect members of Parliament in Nauru (Reilly, 2002).

6.2.2 Voting Criteria

We could easily add to the list of voting rules, but even among these four it is not clear which is best. There are several criteria for deciding which voting rule should be preferred. We introduce six that have been widely used to study collective choice rules (Riker, 1982; Mueller, 2003).

Definition 6.5. *Condorcet winner criterion*: The Condorcet winner, if one exists, is the candidate that beats every other candidate in pairwise comparison using simple majority rule. A voting rule satisfies the Condorcet winner criterion if it chooses the Condorcet winner when one exists.

The Condorcet winner criterion, otherwise known as the Condorcet criterion, is named after the eighteenth century mathematician and philosopher Marquis de Condorcet. Condorcet believed that if any candidate could beat all others in pairwise competition, it ought to be deemed the winner. Keep in mind that each of our four voting rules select equivalent to simple majority rule in two-alternative races. However, the Condorcet winner criterion is really more about picking the winner of every pairwise comparisons than it is about promulgating simple majority rule. Obviously, all four of our voting rules select the Condorcet winner when there are only two candidates because all will be reduced to majority rule in the two-alternative case. Less obvious is that all four can fail to select a Condorcet winner when more than two candidates exist.

Definition 6.6. *Condorcet loser criterion*: The Condorcet loser, if one exists, is the candidate that loses to every other candidate in pairwise comparison using simple majority rule. A voting rule satisfies the Condorcet loser criterion if it does not pick the Condorcet loser when one exists.

A Condorcet loser is a candidate that could never win if paired head-to-head against another candidate. Hence, picking a Condorcet loser is an artificial by-product of considering all the candidates at once and should be avoided. Nurmi (1987) shows that Borda count, MRR, and IRV always avoid a Condorcet loser.[4] In contrast, plurality rule can select Condorcet losers, but that does not mean it often will. Hence, the comparison can still be useful.

Definition 6.7. *Majority criterion*: A majority winner, if one exists, is the candidate that receives the support of more than half of the voters when all candidates are considered at once. A voting rule satisfies the majority criterion if it chooses the majority winner.

Obviously, earning more than half of the vote may be rare. However, if a candidate manages to do so, those who espouse majoritarianism are likely to want to see that candidate selected. Such a candidate receives more first place votes than the rest of the field combined. Plurality rule, MRR, and IRV will always satisfy the majority criterion. The Borda count may not.

Definition 6.8. *Consistency*: If two disjoint subsets of voters V and V' both choose candidate x under voting rule f, then the union of V and V' should also chose x under the same voting rule f.

Young (1974) sees this criterion as a kind of weak Pareto condition applied to subsets of voters. If both subsets of voters agree on a particular candidate, then the full set of voters should select the same candidate. This creates coherence between subsets and unions, which helps avoid certain types of manipulation (Riker, 1982, p. 100). Among the most widely used voting systems, only plurality rule and the Borda count are always consistent (Nurmi, 1987, pp. 100–4). MRR and IRV may select inconsistently.

Definition 6.9. *Reversal symmetry*: if candidate A is the unique winner of an election and then the preferences of each voter are inverted, so their least preferred alternative becomes most preferred, their second least preferred alternative becomes second preferred, etc., then candidate A must not be elected. Electing A violates reversal symmetry (Saari, 1995; Saari and Barney, 2003).

---

[4] Nurmi (1987, p. 54) refers to IRV as the Hare system. Saari (2003, p. 544) shows that the Borda count, MRR, and IRV will avoid such losers when voters are strategic.

To illustrate this criterion, imagine what would happen if the NCAA coaches poll asked coaches to rank football teams in the natural order of most preferred at the top of a list to least preferred at the bottom. Unknown to coaches, the computer program used to tally the rankings had a glitch and considered the rankings in reverse order with the team in the lowest position ranked first, the team in the second lowest position ranked second, etc. The coaches might be angered about the glitch, but they probably would be stunned if they discovered that a voting rule ranked the same team #1 using both preference orders. Such a voting rule would violate reversal symmetry. Although the Borda count can never violate reversal symmetry, it may be surprising to note that plurality rule, MRR, and IRV can.[5]

Definition 6.10. *Independence of eliminated alternatives (IEA)*: A candidate that wins an election with m candidates must not lose the election if another candidate is no longer available.

Consider, for example, a three-way race between candidates a, b, and x. If a wins the election among $\{a, b, x\}$, thereby defeating b, candidate b should not win the election if x can no longer participate. This criterion differs from Arrow's independence of irrelevant alternatives and it is a slightly narrower version of Sen's property-α (1979, 17),[6] The former requires that the social ranking between any two alternatives should be independent of individual rankings between one or more alternatives that are not part of the pair (Arrow, 1951). It does not refer to the addition or elimination of alternatives. All four of our voting rules can violate IEA.

Now that we have introduced our six criteria, the reader might ask "what happened to Pareto?" As noted in Chapter 3, the probability of randomly drawing a Pareto preferred alternative decreases as the number of voters increases. This implies that all alternatives become Pareto optimal in sufficiently large populations. Hence, examining a voting rule's adherence to Pareto optimality or the Pareto criterion in a mass election may not be very useful. In mass elections, with tens of thousands or even millions of voters, the probability that at least one candidates is Pareto suboptimal is extremely small. Furthermore, well reasoned candidates will not want to put themselves in Pareto sub-optimal positions because there would always exist another position that all voters would prefer them to take. Since Pareto sub-optimality is a necessary condition for a Pareto improvement, the Pareto criterion is likely to play a small roll in helping institutional designers evaluate the voting rules used in mass elections.

To drive the point home, consider a single-dimensional spatial voting model which we will employ in this chapter. As noted in Chapter 4, the set of Pareto optimal alternatives in a single-dimensional model ranges from the voter furthest on the left to the voter furthest on the right. At least one candidate must be outside this range in order for a Pareto improvement to exist. Across all of the simulations

---

[5] Saari (1999) shows that, in three candidate elections, Borda count is the only positional method which adheres to reversal symmetry. Plurality rule is the only other positional method studied here.

[6] Sen's property alpha applies to choice sets with one or more elements. IEA, as used here, is limited to cases where the choice set contains a single element.

described in this chapter, the most frequent case of randomly drawing a Pareto sub-optimal outcome was for a population of 10,000 random voters and ten random candidates, both drawn from a normal distribution with a mean of 0.5 and standard deviation of 0.2. In that case, a Pareto sub-optimal outcome was drawn only 1,955 times out of 1 million trials (less than two-tenths of a percent). Furthermore, none of the voting rules choose the Pareto sub-optimal candidate across any of our simulations. Since a single-dimensional framework makes almost all candidates Pareto optimal and all the voting rules we examine never select a Pareto sub-optimal candidate when one exists, the Pareto criterion is of little use for the studying mass elections.

Other criteria, such as transitivity, are omitted because intransitivity is not possible with single-peaked preferences in a single dimension of alternatives. Readers who like the spirit of transitivity might be particularly interested in the results of the Condorcet winner criterion. A Condorcet winner beats all other candidates pairwise and provides electoral stability similar to transitivity.

6.3 Simulations

Although deducing the probability that a voting rule selects a criterion would be more appealing than simulating it, there are two reasons why we simulate probabilities here. First, deducing probabilities can be mathematically difficult, particularly for four voting rules, six criteria, and three assumptions about electoral conditions. Analytical works on the probability of an intransitive social ranking have required decades to develop (Niemi and Weisberg, 1968; Gehrlein, 2002a; Gehrlein and Lepelley, 2010) and even these results require certain assumptions about preference orders. Comparable results for the criteria and conditions examined here cannot be expected overnight. Second, simulations provide fairly good approximations of deductive probabilities and can be modified to reflect conditions that one might expect in actual elections. With recent improvements in computing, more realistic conditions can be studied like large populations of voters and more complex distributions. Both can be accomplished while still requiring a large number of trials.

Studies that have used simulations in a spatial voting framework include Merrill (1984) and Chamberlin and Cohen (1978). Both are limited to an examination of the Condorcet winner criterion and a utilitarian criterion for a slightly different set of voting rules. Other scholars have examined the probability of selecting a Condorcet winner deductively (Van Newenhizen, 1992; Gehrlein, 2002a; Gehrlein and Lepelley, 2010), but not within the context of a single-dimensional model. Nurmi and Uusi-Heikkila (1986) simulate the probability that plurality rule and approval voting produce weak Pareto improvements and Condorcet losers. They assume an impartial culture condition, an unipolar culture condition, and a bipolar culture condition. Each assumption affects the distribution of preferences in the domain. They find that plurality rule is more likely to select a Condorcet loser in a bipolar culture than in an impartial culture, but never compare these results to those for MRR, IRV, and the Borda count. Lepelley (1993) derives the exact probability that plurality rule selects the Condorcet loser under an impartial *anonymous* culture condition, but his proof is limited to three candidates.[7] Because they believe the impartial culture condition and other uniform distributions rarely exist, Nurmi (1992) and Regenwetter et al (2006) criticize the use of the impartial culture condition as an assumption about underlying preferences.

A single-dimensional model, like the one used here, might avoid the latter problem because it has been widely accepted as a good model for elections in the social choice literature. However, a single-dimensional model restricts the set of permissable preferences and affects the probability of selecting a Condorcet winner and Condorcet loser. Whether these results, or the ones derived from assumptions like the impartial culture condition, are more convincing ultimately depends on the plausibility of the preference structure. Since we also examine the majority criterion, consistency, reversal symmetry, and independence of eliminated alternatives, our results seem to extend beyond the literature.[8]

Although our primary tool here will be the simulations, we also prove an analytic result pertaining to the Condorcet winner criterion (see Proposition 8). To the best of our knowledge, this result is new.

6.3.1 Assumptions

Assume that there are N voters with ideal points I_i in a single-dimensional policy space ranging from 0 to 1, inclusive. Each individual has single-peaked and symmetric utility. These assumptions imply that individuals prefer candidates closer to their ideal points to candidates farther away. We consider voter i indifferent between two (or more) candidates if and only if the two (or more) candidates are equally distant from I_i. Although this setting limits the set of admissible preferences and eliminates the possibility of voting cycles, there has been a long tradition of modeling elections using a single-dimensional model (Black, 1948; Downs, 1957; Enelow and Hinich, 1990). Recent empirical studies further suggest that politics may be single-dimensional (Poole and Rosenthal, 1997; McCarty et al, 2005).

We further assume that individuals vote sincerely (i.e., for the candidate closest to them). Although strategic voting may be more realistic, there are several reasons that we assume actors behave sincerely. First, this assumption allows us to use a simple

---

[7] To be precise, the impartial *anonymous* culture condition assumes that each possible *combination* of strict linear preference orders are equally likely. The impartial culture condition assumes that each *permutation* of the strict linear preference orders are equally likely. See Gehrlein and Lepelley (2010) for a more careful discussion of these distinctions.

[8] There is also growing research on the frequency of violating voting criteria in actual elections (Felsenthal et al, 1993; Regenwetter et al, 2006). The clear advantage of such studies is that they can derive probabilities that occur in natural settings. The disadvantage is that only a limited number of preference orders can be observed in any given study and there are problems of measuring preferences. Albeit more abstract, a simulation offers hundreds of thousands of cases for comparison without measurement error.

model that may give a good first approximation to an actual election. Second, sincere voting may be common in elections. The existence of large third parties in countries such as United Kingdom and Canada may be evidence of this. Third, strategic voting is difficult in mass elections. Large numbers of voters typically have to coordinate their behavior for strategic voting to have the desired effect. For example, in the 2000 U.S. Presidential election, voters who favored Ralph Nader first, Al Gore second, and George W. Bush third had a difficult time coordinating a strategic vote for Gore, partly because they wanted to demonstrate some support for their favorite candidate. Fourth, if candidates are allowed to determine their positions strategically, then for a fixed distribution of voters there may be a set of pure strategy equlibria with only m possible positions for the candidates (Palfrey, 1984; Cox, 1987). Even if there were a slightly larger set of possible locations, the lack of variation in candidate positions would prevent the simulations from generating meaningful results.

Each trial in the simulation proceeds by randomly drawing ideal points for $10,000$ voters from a pre-specified distribution on the $[0,1]$ interval. The simulation then draws m candidates ranging from three to ten from another pre-specified distribution. The distribution of candidates may or may not differ from the distribution of voters. In either case, candidates and votes are always limited to the interval $[0,1]$.[9] Distances between the voters and candidates are then determined to create individual preference orders. Distances are not used to measure intensities.

Because indifference causes a number of computational difficulties for the simulation and it should occur with a probability near zero in our spatial model, we remove all indifference from our study. Two types of indifference could occur. The first results if two candidates are drawn at the same location. In those cases our simulation redraws one of the candidates until he/she was at a new location, distinct from all other candidates. The second type of indifference occurs when a voter is an equal distance away from two candidates in different positions (i.e., the voter is halfway between them). In those cases, we resolve the voter's indifference with the flip of a coin. This was operationalized in the simulation by moving the indifferent voter 10^{-10} units to the right or to left with each direction being equally probable. Despite our diligence, these adjustments to our program proved unnecessary. There was never a case of either type of indifference in any of our simulations. Each simulation lasted for 1 million trials.

After individual preferences are determined they are put into an array that mimics a preference list. Each column in the array represents one of the possible preference orders that can occur in that particular trial. The first row of the array contains the number of occurrences of the preference order. The second row through the last row contains an ordering of candidate names with the most preferred candidate listed in the second row and least preferred candidate listed in the last row. Using a preference list such as this makes the application of some of the criteria, such as reversal symmetry and IEA, easier and reduces the number of passes through the $N \times m$ distances. The latter is computationally expensive.

---

[9] In cases where voters or candidates are drawn from outside $[0,1]$, their location was redrawn until it was within $[0,1]$.

The program first records whether the voting rule produces a tie and whether the Condorcet winner, Condorcet loser, majority criterion, or the reversal symmetry criterion[10] failed to recommend a particular candidate in each trial.[11] Such trials are discarded, and the remaining trials are deemed "eligible." Among the eligible trials, the program then records the candidate selected by each voting rule and each criterion separately. If there is a match, we count a success for the voting rule on the criterion in that particular trial.[12] For these four criteria, we report the frequencies of adhering to a given criterion given that the criterion selected a candidate and the voting rule did not tie, i.e., the number of successes divided by the number of eligible trials. In a large number of trials, this frequency should approximate the true probability in the model.

For the consistency criterion the program randomly chooses 100 two-subset partitions of voters. The two subsets formed by each partition may or may not be of equal size. For each partition, the program determines the winner in the two subsets formed by the partition as well as the winner in the full set of voters. We call a partition "eligible" if both subsets make the same selection and neither the full population nor the two subsets produces a tie. Among eligible partitions, a "success" occurs if the subsets choose the same candidate as the full population. We then report the frequency of successes among all eligible partitions. Note that this figure will only be an approximation for the likelihood of consistency, since the consistency principle considers all possible partitions. Numerical evidence suggests that our approximation may be quite accurate. For instance, simulations with only one randomly drawn partition per trial produced very similar data.[13]

Finally, to determine whether a voting rule adheres to the IEA criterion, we record the winners among m candidates for each voting rule, then remove one of the losing candidates and record winners among the remaining $m - 1$ candidates. We then record the number of "eligible samples," i.e. the number of instances where the original election does not tie, and there is no tie after a losing candidate is eliminated from the list. Thus, the total number of eligible samples would be bounded

---

[10] Reversal symmetry always recommends a candidate if the voting rule does not tie (either originally or in the inverted set of preferences).

[11] Ties include cases where more than one candidate is selected or the voting rule does not produce a clear winner. For example, if the three candidates with the most first place votes receive the same number of votes and all other candidates receive no first place votes, plurality, MRR, and IRV will not produce a clear winner (i.e., each produces a tie). Procedures for resolving ties undoubtedly exist, but they vary by region and are not included in the common statements of the voting rules. Rather than adopt one of these regional procedures, we exclude ties to study the properties of the voting rules as they are stated in the formal theory literature. Flipping a coin would alter the probabilities reported without making it clear to the reader by how much.

[12] For the Condorcet loser criterion, successes are counted if the voting rule does not select the Condorcet loser. For reversal symmetry, successes are counted if the voting rule does not select the same candidate after the preference order is reversed.

[13] For our simulation with 100 partitions we also considered reporting frequencies summed over trials alone, where a trial would count as a success only if it was consistent for all eligible cases in that trial (i.e., for all cases among the 100 partitions where the voting rule did not tie and the two subsets selected equivalently). This produced almost identical probabilities as the ones reported in Table 6.1.

above by the number of trials (1 million) times $(m-1)$. If candidate x won the original election and won the election among the remaining $m-1$ candidates, then we count the trial as a success. We repeat this process for each losing candidate in a trial and report the frequency of successes among all eligible samples.[14]

6.4 Results

6.4.1 Condorcet Winner

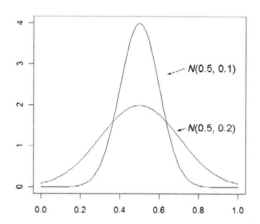

Fig. 6.1 Normal Distribution

Note: In our first simulation voters are normally distributed with a mean of 0.5 and a standard deviation of 0.2. Candidates are normally distributed with a mean of 0.5 and a standard deviation of 0.1.

Simulated results for the Condorcet winner criterion are presented in Table 6.1. The columns correspond to the number of candidates, and the rows correspond to the four voting rules. There are three different sets of distributions. The first, presented on top, draws voters from a normal distribution with mean 0.5 and standard deviation of 0.2. Normal distributions are commonly attributed to countries such as the United States and the United Kingdom. In the same simulation, candidates are drawn from a narrower distribution with mean of 0.5 and standard deviation of 0.1. This reflects the observation that candidates often tend toward the middle of a

---

[14] We also considered reporting frequencies summed over trials alone, where a trial counts as a success only if it adheres to IEA for all eligible samples in that trial. This produced much smaller probabilities. Nevertheless, in terms of performance on the IEA criterion, the rank order of the voting rules remained the same in almost every case.

distribution in order to win an election. These distributions are displayed in Figure 6.1. The second, presented in the middle of the table, draws candidates and from the same distribution — a normal distribution with mean of 0.5 and a standard deviation of 0.2. The third, presented in the bottom of the table, draws voters from a bimodal distribution with modes at 0.25 and 0.75 and a standard deviation of 0.20 for each mode.[15] Candidates are drawn from a similar bimodal distribution. However, they have a smaller standard deviation of 0.10 for each mode. Such a distribution might reflect partisan voting in districts with two parties.

Table 6.1 The probability of selecting a Condorcet winner (10,000 voters)

Voting rule	Number of Candidates			
	3	5	7	10
Distribution: voters $\sim N(0.5, 0.2)$, candidates $\sim N(0.5, 0.1)$				
Plurality	0.516	0.144	0.041	0.007
Majority with runoff	0.574	0.208	0.082	0.024
IRV	0.574	0.221	0.127	0.097
Borda count	0.853	0.791	0.745	0.712
Distribution: voters $\sim N(0.5, 0.2)$, candidates $\sim N(0.5, 0.2)$				
Plurality	0.703	0.430	0.305	0.213
Majority with runoff	0.852	0.666	0.539	0.412
IRV	0.852	0.588	0.437	0.315
Borda count	0.874	0.820	0.779	0.739
Distribution: voters bimodal wide, candidates bimodal narrow				
Plurality	0.547	0.350	0.307	0.317
Majority with runoff	0.845	0.760	0.716	0.705
IRV	0.845	0.670	0.593	0.521
Borda count	0.772	0.707	0.668	0.694

Note: In the third distribution voters are drawn from one of two normal distributions with equal probability, $N(0.25, 0.20)$ and $N(0.75, 0.20)$; candidates are also drawn from one of two normal distributions with equal probability, $N(0.25, 0.10)$ and $N(0.75, 0.10)$. Trials = 1 million.

The numbers reported depict the conditional probability that a voting rule adheres to the criterion given that the criterion made a clear recommendation and the voting rule did not tie. Across 1 million trials, the number of "ties" range from 37 for the Borda count with three candidates to 2,763 for majority rule with a runoff with ten candidates — both of which were from the distributions reported at the bottom of the table. This represents a very small fraction of the total number of trials (slightly more than one-tenth of one percent). Hence, our decision to exclude ties has little effect on the results. Furthermore, the number of Condorcet winners range from

---

[15] This distribution is created by randomly drawing voters from one of two normal distributions, each occurring with equal probability. The first has a mean of 0.25 and standard deviation of 0.20. The second has a mean of 0.75 and standard deviation of 0.20.

999,037 for ten candidates to 999,739 for three candidates, both from the middle of the table. This large number of Condorcet winners (more than 99.9%) facilitates a comparison of voting rules on this criterion. With the exception of the results for the majority criterion (described later), the the standard errors for all criteria, voting rules, and candidates were no greater than 5.0×10^{-4}. Hence, for all cases where the reported difference between any two probabilities is greater than .001, the difference is statistically significant at the .01 level. This applies to both the results reported Table 6.1 and to the results presented later in this chapter.[16]

These figures clearly suggest that plurality rule is the least likely to select the Condorcet winners among the cases presented here. Among the three other voting rules, Borda count is clearly the best for the unimodal distributions centered at .5, whereas MRR performs better for the bimodal distribution on the bottom of the table. Note that all distributions presented in the table are symmetric about .5. We also considered a case where the distributions for both voters and candidates were nonsymmetric, and found that Borda count performed the worst among the four voting rules in this setting, while MRR performed the best.[17]

Our results for the unimodal distributions are fairly consistent with the results reported by Merrill (1984) and Nurmi (1992) for random and impartial culture conditions. Although our results from the bimodal distribution may appear to contradict the results of Van Newenhizen (1992), who proves that Borda count is the most likely voting rule to select a Condorcet winner for a uniform distribution of voter profiles, the differences between our result and hers undoubtedly stems from differences in the distribution of preferences. Hence, the robustness of Van Newenhizen's result to other "uniform-like" probability distributions is worthy of further investigation.

Our numerical results are given some rigorous support by the following proposition.

Proposition 8 *Assume three candidates are randomly and independently chosen from a continuous probability distribution on* $[0, 1]$, *and assume the voters are randomly and independently chosen from a probability distribution on* $[0, 1]$. *Then the probability that the Condorcet winner wins at least half of the first place votes is at least* $1/2$.

Proof. Assume N is odd, so that a median voter is unique. The proof for N even can be shown similarly. Let V be the location of the median voter. Suppose A is both the name and the location of the Condorcet winner, and B and C are the names and locations of the other two candidates. Also assume for the moment that $A > V$. The proof for $A < V$ is similar, and $A = V$ occurs with probability zero. Note that A is a Condorcet winner if and only if A is closer to V than both B and C.

Claim: The probability that B, C are either both greater than or both less than A, given that A is the Condorcet winner, is at least $1/2$.

---

[16] Some of the figures reported in Tables 6.4 and 6.6 differ by only .001, but were also significant at the .01 level.

[17] In this simulation voters were randomly drawn with equal probability from one of two normal distributions: $N(.10, .05)$ and $N(.50, .05)$ and candidates were drawn from $N(.2, .1)$

Proof of claim: The fact that A is the Condorcet winner (acw) implies that B, C must be restricted to either $[0, 2V - A)$ or $(A, 1]$. Suppose the probability that a candidate is chosen in $[0, 2V - A)$ (resp. $(A, 1]$) given that acw, is α_1 (resp. α_2). Then by independence in the selection of B and C, which remains in effect for the conditional probabilities here, the following formulae hold:

$$Pr((B < A) \cap (C < A)|acw) = \alpha_1^2,$$

$$Pr((B > A) \cap (C > A)|acw) = \alpha_2^2,$$

$$Pr(B < A < C|acw) = Pr(C < B < A|acw) = \alpha_1 \alpha_2.$$

Note that the four probabilities listed above must add up to one, so the claim now follows from the following inequality:

$$\alpha_1^2 + \alpha_2^2 \geq 2\alpha_1 \alpha_2,$$

which follows immediately from $(\alpha_1 - \alpha_2)^2 \geq 0$.

We now claim that in all cases where either $B, C < A$ or $B, C > A$, A will always win more than half of the first place votes. To prove the claim, suppose on one hand that $B, C > A$. Since $A > V$, all voters on the interval $[0, A]$ will vote for A. Because this interval contains V, A will certainly win more than half of the first place votes in this case. On the other hand, suppose $B, C < A$. Because A is the Condorcet winner and $V < A$, it follows that all the voters on the interval $[V, 1]$ will vote for A. Because this interval contains V, A will again win more than half of the first place votes. $\square$

Corollary 2 *Assume the hypotheses of Proposition 8. Then Condorcet winners will be selected by plurality, MRR, and IRV with probability at least $1/2$.*

Two key facts in the proof of Proposition 8 are (i) when the Condorcet winner either has all opponents to her left or all opponents to her right, then she will always win at least half the voters, and (ii) this positioning will take place at least half of the time. For $m > 3$, the first fact remains true, but the second does not. With more candidates, it is increasing likely that the Condorcet winner will have opponents both on her left and on her right. This explains why the probability of selecting a Condorcet winner decreases as $m - 1$ increases for the first three voting rules in Table 6.1.

Furthermore, Proposition 8 proves that a Condorcet winner is certain to receive more than half of the first place votes if her opponents are both to her left or both to her right. In contrast we can show that the winner of the Borda count is most likely to be the Condorcet winner when one opponent is on her left and the other is on her right. Borda count can do poorly in cases where the Condorcet winner is on one side of the median, and her two opponents are on the other side.[18] The reasons

---

[18] A weak analogue of Proposition 8 can be proven for the Borda count with $m = 3$. If the probability distributions for both the candidates and the voters are symmetric about .5, and if $V = .5$, then with probability .5 the Condorcet winner will lie between the other two candidates, and in these cases the Borda count will select the Condorcet winner. The assumption about the proba-

for this are somewhat technical, but can be summarized as follows. The candidate that lies between the other two candidates, which we label x, will pick up only first and second place votes, whereas the Condorcet winner in this case will pick up some third place votes. If there is a large segment of the population that ranks x first (and thus awards three points per voter to x) and the Condorcet winner last (and thus awards only one point per voter to the Condorcet winner), then the gains x makes in this segment of the population will overcome the advantages enjoyed by the Condorcet winner. A careful analysis shows that this is often the case for the bimodal distribution in Table 6.1, which partly explains why the Borda count does relatively poorly in this setting.

It is also interesting to note that our voting rules are more likely to select Condorcet winners when candidates and voters are drawn from the same normal distribution (middle case) than when candidates are drawn from a narrower distribution (top case). This might suggest that electoral incentives that drive candidates to the center of a distribution may actually reduce the probability of selecting Condorcet winners.

6.4.2 Condorcet Loser

Results for the Condorcet loser criterion are reported in Table 6.2. In this case, the number of Condorcet losers range from $999,174$ cases for ten candidates in the distribution depicted on the bottom of Table 6.2, to $999,811$ cases for three candidates in the distribution depicted in the middle of Table 6.2. Again, the large number of Condorcet losers (more than 99.9% of the trials) helps facilitate a comparison between the voting rules on this criterion. Figures reported are the probabilities that a voting rule *avoids* a Condorcet loser given that one exists and the voting rule did not tie.

Because it has been shown that MRR, IRV, and the Borda count always avoid a Condorcet loser (Nurmi, 1987), the most interesting results is that plurality rule is likely to avoid the Condorcet loser as well. This illustrates the value of comparing the probability that a voting rule will adhere to a criterion, when it is known that other voting rules always will. Even though plurality rule can select Condorcet losers, it infrequently does.

Nevertheless, the differences we report for plurality and the other three voting rules are statistically significant. If someone finds the Condorcet loser criterion particularly troubling, then they may have reason to avoid plurality rule. If they favor plurality rule for other reasons and find the Condorcet loser criterion only a moderate concern, then they might conclude that plurality rule does not perform a whole lot differently than the other three voting rules.

---

bility distributions, though restrictive, will be satisfied by the distributions displayed in Table 6.1. With 10,000 voters and a reasonably large population density in a neighborhood of .5, the median voter will be very close to .5, and thus the Condorcet winner will lie between the other two candidates (and hence win the Borda count) with a probability very close to .5.

Table 6.2 The probability of selecting a Condorcet loser (10,000 voters)

Voting rule	Number of Candidates			
	3	5	7	10
Distribution: voters $\sim N(0.5, 0.2)$, candidates $\sim N(0.5, 0.1)$				
Plurality	0.874	0.887	0.890	0.893
Majority with runoff	1.000	1.000	1.000	1.000
IRV	1.000	1.000	1.000	1.000
Borda count	1.000	1.000	1.000	1.000
Distribution: voters $\sim N(0.5, 0.2)$, candidates $\sim N(0.5, 0.2)$				
Plurality	0.934	0.965	0.975	0.983
Majority with runoff	1.000	1.000	1.000	1.000
IRV	1.000	1.000	1.000	1.000
Borda count	1.000	1.000	1.000	1.000
Distribution: voters bimodal wide, candidates bimodal narrow				
Plurality	0.800	0.921	0.958	0.972
Majority with runoff	1.000	1.000	1.000	1.000
IRV	1.000	1.000	1.000	1.000
Borda count	1.000	1.000	1.000	1.000

Note: In the third distribution voters are drawn from one of two normal distributions with equal probability, $N(0.25, 0.20)$ and $N(0.75, 0.20)$; candidates are also drawn from one of two normal distributions with equal probability, $N(0.25, 0.10)$ and $N(0.75, 0.10)$. Trials = 1 million.

In comparison to previous works, plurality rule selects a Condorcet loser at a slightly lower rate than the probabilities derived by Lepelley (1993) and simulated by Nurmi and Uusi-Heikkila (1986). Lepelley calculated the probability that plurality rule selects a Condorcet loser in three-candidate elections assuming the impartial *anonymous* culture condition. Nurmi and Uusi-Heikkilä simulated these probabilities for three to five candidates, in an impartial anonymous culture condition, an unipolar culture condition, and a bipolar culture condition with 40 voters or less. Our results offer some robustness to these studies while suggesting that a single-dimensional model may dampen the performance of plurality rule slightly. It also extends the results to elections with more candidates and larger populations of voters.

6.4.3 Majority Criterion

Table 6.3 presents the results for the majority criterion. Unlike the previous two criteria, the number of times a candidate receives support from the majority of the population when all candidates are considered simultaneously is much smaller, particularly for cases with a large numbers of candidates. For $m = 3$ there are roughly a half-million cases where a majority of voters prefer one candidate as their first place

Table 6.3 The probability of adhering to the majority criterion (10,000 voters)

Voting rule	Number of Candidates			
	3	5	7	10
Distribution: voters $\sim N(0.5, 0.2)$, candidates $\sim N(0.5, 0.1)$				
Plurality	1.000	1.000	1.000	1.000
Majority with runoff	1.000	1.000	1.000	1.000
IRV	1.000	1.000	1.000	1.000
Borda count	0.706	0.413	0.285	0.183
Distribution: voters $\sim N(0.5, 0.2)$, candidates $\sim N(0.5, 0.2)$				
Plurality	1.000	1.000	1.000	1.000
Majority with runoff	1.000	1.000	1.000	1.000
IRV	1.000	1.000	1.000	1.000
Borda count	0.782	0.510	0.353	0.205
Distribution: voters bimodal wide, candidates bimodal narrow				
Plurality	1.000	1.000	1.000	1.000
Majority with runoff	1.000	1.000	1.000	1.000
IRV	1.000	1.000	1.000	1.000
Borda count	0.544	0.462	0.390	0.294

Note: In the third distribution voters are drawn from one of two normal distributions with equal probability, $N(0.25, 0.20)$ and $N(0.75, 0.20)$; candidates are also drawn from one of two normal distributions with equal probability, $N(0.25, 0.10)$ and $N(0.75, 0.10)$. Trials = 1 million.

choice across all three sets of distributions, roughly half the number of trials. For $m = 10$ there were roughly 3,900 cases, less than one percent of the trials. Nevertheless, for the majority criterion standard errors are 7.3×10^{-3} or less in all of the cases reported. This implies that the difference in proportions between the Borda count and the other three voting rules is significant at the .01 level for all the figures reported.

Of course, plurality rule, MRR, and IRV will always select a majority winner when one exists. It is also well-known that the Borda count may not. The interesting finding from these results is how poorly the Borda count performs compared to the other three voting rules, particularly for a large number of candidates. If there are ten candidates and individuals are drawn from the distributions depicted on the top part of Table 6.3, then the Borda count will miss a majority winner more than four out every five times one occurs. It might also be noted that Borda count tends to underperform the other three voting rules more on the majority criterion than it overperforms the other three voting rules on either the Condorcet winner or the Condorcet loser criterion.

6.4.4 Consistency

Table 6.4 The probability of maintaining consistency (10,000 voters)

Voting rule	Number of Candidates			
	3	5	7	10
Distribution: voters $\sim N(0.5, 0.2)$, candidates $\sim N(0.5, 0.1)$				
Plurality	1.000	1.000	1.000	1.000
Majority with runoff	1.000	1.000	1.000	1.000
IRV	1.000	1.000	0.998	0.994
Borda count	1.000	1.000	1.000	1.000
Distribution: voters $\sim N(0.5, 0.2)$, candidates $\sim N(0.5, 0.2)$				
Plurality	1.000	1.000	1.000	1.000
Majority with runoff	1.000	1.000	1.000	1.000
IRV	1.000	0.999	0.998	0.993
Borda count	1.000	1.000	1.000	1.000
Distribution: voters bimodal wide, candidates bimodal narrow				
Plurality	1.000	1.000	1.000	1.000
Majority with runoff	1.000	1.000	1.000	0.999
IRV	1.000	0.999	0.998	0.991
Borda count	1.000	1.000	1.000	1.000

Note: The frequency of cases adhering to consistency are summed over 1 million trials and 100 partitions. In the third distribution voters are drawn from one of two normal distributions with equal probability, $N(0.25, 0.20)$ and $N(0.75, 0.20)$; candidates are also drawn from one of two normal distributions with equal probability, $N(0.25, 0.10)$ and $N(0.75, 0.10)$.

Results for the consistency criterion are reported in Table 6.4. Recall that consistency requires that if two subsets of the voting population select the same unique candidate x, then the union of the two subsets should also select x. The number of cases where the two subsets pick the same candidate and there are no ties varies by distribution, the number of candidates, and the voting rule. The percentage of the 100 million possible comparisons exceeded 70%, with the smallest percentage from IRV in the bimodal distribution with 10 candidates. The large number of comparable cases is largely due to the fact that randomly partitioning 10,000 voters into two sets will often produce very similar distributions.

It can be shown that plurality rule and the Borda count will always be consistent, whereas MRR and IRV may not. What is interesting about these results is that each of the voting rules maintain consistency with large probabilities. MRR almost always selects consistently. IRV selects consistently at least 99% of the time. With all of our voting rules performing so well on this criterion, one might be tempted to conclude that we should not worry about consistency. Unfortunately, these figures are likely to overstate the true rates of consistency because only 100 partitions are considered for any given set of individual preference orders.[19] If all possible partitions were considered, there might be more cases of inconsistency. Nevertheless, the probabilities are high and the differences in performance between MRR, IRV, and the two voting rules that can never violate consistency appear trivial.

6.4.5 Reversal Symmetry

Table 6.5 The probability of adhering to reversal symmetry (10,000 voters)

Voting rule	Number of Candidates			
	3	5	7	10
Distribution: voters $\sim N(0.5, 0.2)$, candidates $\sim N(0.5, 0.1)$				
Plurality	0.874	0.887	0.890	0.893
Majority with runoff	1.000	1.000	1.000	1.000
IRV	1.000	1.000	1.000	1.000
Borda count	1.000	1.000	1.000	1.000
Distribution: voters $\sim N(0.5, 0.2)$, candidates $\sim N(0.5, 0.2)$				
Plurality	0.934	0.965	0.975	0.983
Majority with runoff	1.000	1.000	1.000	0.991
IRV	1.000	1.000	1.000	1.000
Borda count	1.000	1.000	1.000	1.000
Distribution: voters bimodal wide, candidates bimodal narrow				
Plurality	0.800	0.921	0.958	0.972
Majority with runoff	1.000	1.000	1.000	1.000
IRV	1.000	1.000	1.000	1.000
Borda count	1.000	1.000	1.000	1.000

Note: In the third distribution voters are drawn from one of two normal distributions with equal probability, $N(0.25, 0.20)$ and $N(0.75, 0.20)$; candidates are also drawn from one of two normal distributions with equal probability, $N(0.25, 0.10)$ and $N(0.75, 0.10)$. Trials = 1 million.

Results for the reversal symmetry criterion are displayed in Table 6.5. Because reverse symmetry always recommends a candidate whenever there is not a tie, reversal symmetry recommended a winner in at least 99.9% of the trials reported. This is a large number of cases for comparison.

Perhaps the most striking result is that plurality rule, MRR, and IRV are all capable of violating reversal symmetry. Yet in our simulation, IRV violated reversal symmetry at most 70 out of 1 million trials — in the simulation with three candidates and a bimodal distribution. MRR never violated reversal symmetry. Most

---

[19] We restrict ourselves to 100 two-subset partitions because of limitations in computational hours. All possible two-subset partitions of 10,000 voters would be astronomically large.

readers should find the differences between IRV, on the one hand, and MRR and the Borda count, on the other, so negligible that the voting rules should be treated as performing equally on this criterion. In contrast, plurality rule was clearly the weakest performer. But even the differences between it and the perfect performance of the Borda count may seem negligible in some contexts — particularly for elections with a large number of candidates.

6.4.6 Independence of Eliminated Alternatives (IEA)

Table 6.6 The probability of adhering to IEA (10,000 voters)

Voting rule	Number of Candidates			
	3	5	7	10
Distribution: voters $\sim N(0.5, 0.2)$, candidates $\sim N(0.5, 0.1)$				
Plurality	0.411	0.533	0.612	0.682
Majority with runoff	0.634	0.721	0.764	0.798
IRV	0.634	0.557	0.517	0.489
Borda count	0.807	0.849	0.872	0.877
Distribution: voters $\sim N(0.5, 0.2)$, candidates $\sim N(0.5, 0.2)$				
Plurality	0.527	0.569	0.613	0.664
Majority with runoff	0.639	0.679	0.706	0.729
IRV	0.639	0.638	0.620	0.584
Borda count	0.782	0.886	0.897	0.895
Distribution: voters bimodal wide, candidates bimodal narrow				
Plurality	0.411	0.533	0.612	0.682
Majority with runoff	0.634	0.721	0.764	0.798
IRV	0.634	0.557	0.517	0.489
Borda count	0.807	0.849	0.872	0.877

Note: In the third distribution voters are drawn from one of two normal distributions with equal probability, $N(0.25, 0.20)$ and $N(0.75, 0.20)$; candidates are also drawn from one of two normal distributions with equal probability, $N(0.25, 0.10)$ and $N(0.75, 0.10)$. Trials = 1 million.

Finally, Table 6.6 reports results for the IEA criterion. Because a voting rule meets the conditions for an IEA comparison as long as it does not tie, IEA recommends a winner in more than 99% of the $(m-1) \times 1$ million cases.

We found that all four of our criteria can, and did, violate IEA. However, the Borda count outperforms the other three voting rules for all of the simulations reported in Table 6.6. The worst performer depends upon the conditions. For elections with five or fewer candidates, IRV outperforms plurality rule. For elections with seven to ten candidates, plurality rule outperforms IRV. Furthermore, for three candidates MRR and IRV perform identically, as one should expect. But as the number of candidates increases, IRV's ability to select the same candidate when a loser is eliminated decreases while MRR's independence from eliminated candidates increases. This suggest MRR may be the better of the two voting rules in terms of the IEA criterion. We conclude that in terms of IEA, the Borda count is best followed by MRR. The third best depends on the number of candidates in the election.

6.5 Conclusion

So which voting rule is best? One way of interpreting the various "impossibility" results is to suggest that there is no ideal voting rule for every configuration of preferences. Instead, some types of voting rules work well for some types of choices, while others work well for other types of choices. In this vein, our answer to the question of "which voting rule is best" depends upon the properties valued by a community. If a community wants to chose among the four voting rules analyzed in this chapter, perhaps because three of them have been widely used in single-member districts, and they value the IEA criterion, then it might have reason to prefer Borda count. The Borda count is not widely used in national elections, but our results suggest that it clearly outperforms the other voting rules on this criterion and performs well on the Condorcet loser criterion, consistency, and reversal symmetry. It also outperforms the other voting rules in terms of Condorcet winners if the distribution is unimodal and symmetric.

However, if the same community values the majority criterion, then they might have reason to avoid the Borda count and use MRR instead. MRR performs well on the majority criterion, while avoiding Condorcet losers, maintaining consistency, and adhering to reversal symmetry. Its almost perfect performance on the latter two criteria is a notable finding. Also notable is the ability of MRR to outperform Borda count on the Condorcet winner criterion for bimodal distributions.

Ironically, the one voting rule that seems to be the worst is plurality rule, yet plurality rule is the most widely used voting rule in a single member district. Hence, institutional framers in the United States, Great Britain, India, and other countries may have the most to gain from reflecting on these results.

Saari (2008, p. 214) argues that "those negative social choice results that are consistently being discovered ... should be treated only as first steps toward identifying reasonable starting points for more extensive research investigations." He continues: "In order for a field to prosper and expand, it must offer something of value, a sense of guidance for others." In addition to helping social choice expand by providing quantified comparisons between voting rules that violate a criterion over an unrestricted domain, our results also help social choice expand where one voting rule has been proven to adhere to a criterion while others have been shown to violate it.

In particular, our results the Condorcet loser, reversal symmetry, and consistency criteria give several examples where one voting rule always adheres to a criterion, and another voting rule *almost* always adheres. Arguably the difference is negligible, so an institutional framer may have reason to treat the two voting rules as performing equally well on that criterion.[20] This illustrates the usefulness of comparing probabilities when an axiomatic result may already be known, and shows how social choice can progress despite its many impossibility results.

It is also interesting to note that practically all of comparisons are among candidates within the Pareto optimal set. This is because randomly drawing a large number of voters in a finite space implies that candidates almost always will be Pareto optimal. The problem is only exacerbated if candidates move toward the center of the spectrum. Hence, any theorists who believe that only Paretian judgements are compelling while all other judgements are "arbitrary," must be stripped of all the tools they use for judgement. They can make no judgements between the voting rules used in elections, despite the fact that different voting rules often chose differently. Although we find the Pareto criterion enormously compelling, it is the positive property of failing to differentiate candidates in large voting populations that forces us to move beyond Pareto.

---

[20] It is possible, however, that the "exceptional cases" from the simulations might arise often in real life. Whether this is the case is worthy of further study.

Chapter 7
Conclusion

Roughly a half-century has passed since *The Calculus of Consent* was first published. Yet the questions raised by Buchanan and Tullock's pioneering book seem to be more relevant today than they were in 1962. The spread of democracy, advances in technology, and population growth have increased the demand for new constitutions. Since *The Calculus of Consent* was written, more than half of the 160 countries in the world have thrown out their old constitution and adopted an entirely new one. Some have done so more than once (Goldwin and Kaufman, 1988, p. vii).

Many provincial and local governments have re-constituted their governments and a countless number of home owner associations, governing boards, and local clubs have adopted new covenants, charters, and written agreements. Some national constitutions were written for new countries, but a surprising number were written for enduring nations, such as Spain, Portugal, Turkey, and Greece (Goldwin and Kaufman, 1988). Hence, understanding the development of good constitutional design and the effects of constitutions on political outcomes seems as important today as it was in 1787 when the framers of the U.S. Constitution replaced the nation's first constitution, the Articles of Confederation, with the world's longest-lasting constitution.

With so many new constitutions being created, it would not be a surprise if those writing a covenant, charter, or constitution would look toward experts for some advice. The lessons taught in *The Calculus of Consent* include the notion that voting rules matter and that one should not assume majority rule is always best. The voting rule that a community ought to adopt depends on the context. Constitutional decisions, legislative decisions, and, in our case, electoral decisions often require different methods. The former should be guided by first principles, while the latter two can be chosen by members of the community. Additionally, constitutional decisions and legislative decisions are often made using k-majority rules. This is partly because decision makers in these phases want the opportunity to raise new alternatives as they occur, they want to determine whether a new idea has sufficient support in comparison to the previous idea, and they usually have more time to consider alternatives in a series than the electorate.

In contrast, electoral decisions require expediency, a narrower set of alternatives, and often a vote over a full list candidates all at once. These factors typically lead to different types of voting rules. Furthermore, constitutional decisions often differ from legislative decisions by the importance of decision costs. Constitutional framers may find decision costs negligible, not because they do not exist, but because the external costs produced by the institutions they create are so important. In contrast, legislators who make daily decisions may find decision costs a serious concern.

Buchanan and Tullock's book was successful partly because it suggested that one size does not fit all. The most appropriate voting rule not only depends on the phase of decision making (constitutional, legislative, or electoral), it also depends on the values of each individual in a society and the conditions under which a society exists. A constitution that is good for one society in one setting may be inappropriate for another. Instead, Buchanan and Tullock argue that good constitutional design stems from process. In particular, they advocate a process that helps each society determine the best set of institutions for itself.

7.1 New Themes

We agree with all these lessons. We also agree that sound democracy should not start with majority rule by assumption. If majority rule is to be the centerpiece of democracy, then the desirable properties of majority rule have to be shown. Buchanan and Tullock argued that unanimity rule has certain properties, most notably the prevention of coercive acts against one's will, that make it ideal. In this sense, they replaced majority rule as the centerpiece of democracy with unanimity rule. Deviations from unanimity rule are deemed desirable, but only in cases where decision costs are sufficiently large. In contrast, we show that majority rule also has some basic properties that constitutional framers may want to consider.

In Chapter 4, titled "Constitutional Decision Making," we confirm Buchanan and Tullock's intuition that unanimity rule is particularly adept at selecting outcomes that are both Pareto optimal and Pareto preferred to the initial status quo. If actors vote and propose strategically (or sincerely), then unanimity rule is at least as likely to select outcomes that are Pareto optimal and Pareto preferred to the status quo as other k-majority rules. If proposals are random, then, with rare exceptions, unanimity rule is typically more likely than majority rule to select outcomes that are Pareto preferred to the initial status quo and Pareto optimal. Since Pareto optimality is a natural extension for anyone interested in the Pareto criterion, these results seems particularly germane for those who have been fully persuaded by Buchanan and Tullock's theory.

Nevertheless, Buchanan and Tullock did make statements that loosely connect unanimity rule to Pareto optimality without reference to Pareto improvements from the initial status quo (Buchanan and Tullock, 1962, pp. 94, 171–180; Buchanan, 1967; Tullock, 1998, pp. 106, 122–123). This prompted us to also consider the relationship between various k-majority rules and Pareto optimality without requiring the additional condition related to the initial status quo. That relationship is much more surprising because it seems to produce very different results from the traditional spatial voting literature. The spatial voting literature suggests that the Pareto set and the unanimity rule core are equivalent. In other words, all Pareto optimal outcomes are in equilibrium under unanimity rule and all unanimity rule equilibria are Pareto optimal. This reinforces a close connection between unanimity rule and Pareto optimality. At the same time, the multidimensional spatial voting literature shows that majority rule typically has no equilibrium (i.e., the majority rule core is empty). Some have interpreted this to mean that majority rule can produce just about anything, including Pareto sub-optimal outcomes (Riker, 1980).

By modeling the proposal process and allowing alternatives to start outside the core, we arrive at very different conclusions than traditionally asserted in the spatial voting literature. First, if proposals are generated randomly, then majority rule is almost always more likely to select a Pareto optimal outcome than unanimity rule. Second, if individuals propose sincerely, then any k-majority rule, with $k < N$ is at least as likely to select a Pareto optimal outcome as unanimity rule ($k = N$). Third, if individuals propose strategically and an "attainable minimum" exists in the final round, then the subgame perfect equilibrium under any k-majority rule is Pareto optimal. If an "attainable minimum" does not exist for $k < N$, then unanimity rule will select a Pareto optimal outcome in subgame perfect equilibrium, and other k-majority rules should produce outcomes that are in the Pareto set or extremely close to the Pareto set. In other words, if Pareto optimality is the goal, then majority rule might regain its central position in democratic theory.[1]

With regard to legislative decisions, Buchanan and Tullock argued that decision costs decrease and external costs increase gradually as k increases. In their several publications where they drew these functions, they always seemed to depict two quadratic functions, with gentle slopes. Scholars who have extended their works have started with similar shapes. We argue that these simple notions can be misleading. In our model, both the decision cost function and the external cost function depend on the probability of passage, which is almost constant for k near 0 and k near N, and which has almost all the decrease in the probability of passage taking place over a short interval. This produces very different shapes for the external costs and decision cost functions and very different implications for the optimal k-majority rule. The logistic-type shape of the probability of passage can produce flat regions in the external cost function for the smallest and largest k. Hence, even if we only use external costs to evaluate the optimal k-majority rule, there is often a range of k-majority rules, near unanimity rule, that are optimal. This again questions whether unanimity rule should be given the role as some type of *unique* democratic ideal. In such cases, unanimity rule would be one of many optimal rules, not a singleton.[2]

---

[1] Our results on Pareto optimality should also be useful for studying legislative decisions.

[2] For large values of $p_{1,1}$ the flat spot near N may be very small. If $p_{1,1}$ is completely unknown, a constitutional framer may still want to favor unanimity rule.

If decision costs are germane to the decision, then a variety of other factors affect the optimal k-majority rule. First, it is possible in some settings that decision costs dwarf external costs. In this case, a less inclusive voting role (or even a nonvoting arrangement such as "dictator" or "director") might be preferred. Constitutional provisions for decision making in times of war may reflect such a concern. If external costs and decision costs are equally important, that is neither one is negligible compared to the other, then other factors will affect the optimal k-majority rule.

For example, the homogeneity of the society, as depicted by the initial preference probabilities $p_{1,1}$ and $p_{-1,1}$ can affect the optima. Everything else equal, societies should consider setting their k-majority rule to the number near $k = p_{1,1}N$. If a society is extremely homogenous, then $p_{1,1}$ will be large and more inclusive k-majority rules might be appropriate. If society is particularly heterogenous, then $p_{1,1}$ will be small and a less inclusive k-majority rule may be appropriate.

With decision costs included, the optimal k-majority rule also depends upon the ability to create increasingly desirable proposals between rounds. If the political dynamics are such that the probability of passing a proposal quickly increases with each round, then large k-majority rules may be preferred. Such rules inhibit proposals that hurt minorities in early rounds without amassing large decision costs — due to the rapid improvement of proposals between rounds. However, if proposals do not become more likely to pass in subsequent rounds (or they improve only slowly), then institutional framers might have reason to favor smaller k-majorities near $k = p_{1,1}N$ again.

With regard to elections, Buchanan and Tullock briefly argue that k-majority rules might be used to elect public officials. We point out that k-majority rules are rarely used in elections because many elections do not have a status quo candidate. Even if they did, institutional framers would typically want electoral rules that remained neutral among the candidates and was decisive. This implies a different set of voting rules for elections.

We analyze three voting rules that are widely used to elect representatives in single-member districts and a fourth, the Borda count, which has received recent attention in the social choice literature. Again, we find that the best voting rule depends upon the properties valued by a community. If a community wants to chose among the four voting rules analyzed in this chapter and they value the IEA criterion, then the community might have strong reasons to prefer the Borda count. The Borda count outperforms the other three voting rules on the IEA criterion and performs at least as well on the Condorcet loser criterion, consistency, and reversal symmetry. The Borda Count is the best rule for choosing a Condorcet winner in some cases, but the worst in other cases.

If a community values the majority criterion and wants a voting rule that almost always avoids Condorcet losers, maintains consistency, and adheres to reversal symmetry, then it might have reason to use MRR instead. MRR performs perfectly, or almost perfectly on the latter three criteria despite the fact that it can violate consistency and reversal symmetry. It also performs the best on the Condorcet winner criterion in those cases where the Borda count performs the worst. Plurality rule has the advantage of being simpler and cheaper to administer than the other three voting rules. However, in comparison to the other voting rules, it does not perform particularly well on any of the six criteria. Thus, even though majority rule has some properties that make it desirable in constitutional and legislative settings, the closely related concept of plurality rule may not be desirable for elections. Other modifications, such as combining majority rule with a runoff would probably be considered improvements.

7.2 Pareto Principles as Tools for Judgement

We have placed the Pareto criterion in the center of our analysis because the principle is central to Buchanan and Tullock's analysis and we wanted to formalize and extend parts of their earlier work. As a result, Pareto principles play a crucial role in our Chapters 3, 4, and 5. Accepting these principles has profound effects on the alleged merits of the voting rules analyzed. In Chapter 3 we made a careful distinction between various types of Pareto principles and argued against judging Pareto indeterminant cases in favor of the status quo. In Chapter 4, we analyzed the ability of various k-majority rules to select Pareto optimal outcomes and outcomes that are both Pareto preferred to the initial status quo and Pareto optimal. The use of Pareto criterion in Chapter 5 was much more subtle. We argued that external costs could be measured in terms of expected BT loss. In other words, an external cost would occur only if someone was made worse off by *changing from the status quo to another state of the world*. These were the types of external costs Buchanan and Tullock described in their book.

Nevertheless, we might get very different results if we were to step away from this tradition and think of external costs neutrally with potential loss from both *forcing* individuals to change to another policy and from *preventing* individuals from changing to another policy. In other words, one could argue that we should consider a status quo that makes a number of individuals worse off in comparison to a proposal as something that contains external costs.

For example, an assembly may be asked to eliminate $1 billion of pork barrel spending being currently spent on a bridge to nowhere. Maintaining the status quo on such a project would cause large external costs for taxpayers who would have to pay for the pork, but who would not find provision of the bridge a good use of their money. If the goal is to make the pork barrel spending go away, then arguably the external costs from the bridge are more likely to remain as k increases — in which case, the expected external cost function might increase as k increases, rather than decrease as traditionally argued.

If we include both expected losses from undesirable proposals (the traditional notion) and expected losses from undesirable status quos (the idea introduced now), then we might get very different results than those reported in Chapter 5. The new criterion might be based on something similar to the expected social gain criterion, which we have described as an ordinal version of utilitarianism in another work (Dougherty and Edward, 2010a).

Furthermore, there is a subtle aspect of political philosophy lurking behind our debate between Pareto optimality on the one hand and Pareto optimality and Pareto superiority to the initial status quo on the other. Both criteria contain Pareto optimality, which suggests that a Pareto suboptimal alternative should be avoided. Hence, the choice between these two criteria centers on whether a Pareto improvement from the initial status quo should also be demanded. If everyone votes according to their preferences, then this criterion is very similar to requiring unanimous consent for change. Many modern political philosophers argued that such a principle is necessary for the adoptions of a social contract. For example, Hobbes argues that "[t]he right of all sovereigns is derived originally from the consent of everyone of those that are to be governed" ([1651] 1962, Ch. 42, p. 416). In Locke's words "Men being ... by nature all free, equal, and independent, no one can be put out of this estate and subjected to the political power of another without his own consent" ([1690] 1988, Section 95, p. 330). Both notions of consent seem to support the idea that desirable outcomes should be judged as Pareto improvements from the status quo. In the absence of explicit or implicit consent, changes cannot be considered improvements.

However, other philosophers and legal scholars have argued that free and desirable choice depends on the conditions under which a decision is made. If individuals make a choice under duress, then their choice cannot be considered free. McGann (2006) argues that the same logic applies to social contract theorists (also see Rae, 1975). For Locke, resources are bountiful in the state of nature. Individuals eat what they want and mix their labor with property to call it their own. Locke suggests that individuals will consent to a minimal government that protects property rights under these conditions. For Hobbes, resources are scarce in the state of nature, so scarce that man is in a war of all against all. Under these conditions, individuals are willing to surrender their right to all things and impose an absolute sovereign to protect them from each other. In both of these cases, individuals give their unanimous consent to very different types of governments. McGann (2006) argues that the social contract that individuals are willing to accept depends upon the state of nature (the status quo) from which individuals are forced to make their judgement. Individuals might unanimously agree to surrender their rights to an absolute sovereign rather than fight it out in the state of nature, not because they would freely chose a sovereign with absolute authority, but because Hobbes has imagined a state of nature so awful that individuals would chose absolute monarchy over this abysmal state. In this sense individuals are not making a free choice, any more than an individual is making a free choice under duress. They are offering their consent conditioned upon the alternative imposed if they did not make this choice. If the status quo is abhorrent, they may make very different choices than if the status quo is reasonable.

The argument speaks to the claim that all normatively desirable actions *must* be compared against the status quo. If there is a reasonable status quo and the only harm comes from coercive collective action, then demanding a Pareto improvement may be desirable. This may be the case in a small community deciding whether to incorporate for the first time. However, if the status quo is unjust, so might be the requirement that all constitutional changes must be Pareto improvements from the status quo. This may be a particular important for constitutions that are created to replace the imbalances of a previous regime, as in the transition from autocracy to democracy. For example, the current constitution of Poland was adopted in 1997. Many of its clauses attempt to rectify the wrongs of the communists. In response to communist-era collective farming, Article 23 establishes family farms as the basis of the agricultural economy; Article 39 prohibits forced medical experimentation; and Article 59 acknowledges the right to form trade unions. It is very unlikely that these provisions made those running collective farms, forcing people into medical experiments, or directing resources through the economy better off.

Does this mean that these provisions cannot be considered improvements over the previous state of affairs? Demanding that Pareto improvements are *necessary* for change suggests that either the losers have to be compensated, so that a Pareto improvement is made, or the status quo has to be maintained. But even advocates of Pareto improvements are unlikely to favor compensating some Polish version of Josef Mengele who loses in the transition from a communist regime that allows him to conduct human experiments to a democratic regime that will not tolerate such behavior — in which case, they might question the universal applicability of demanding Pareto improvements from the status quo.

Pareto optimality alone, without the additional requirement of Pareto superiority to the initial status quo, does not suffer the same fate. Pareto optimality is not conditioned upon any particular status quo — real or hypothetical. It is a comparison between all feasible states of the world, and it remains neutral with respect to all alternatives. Hence, the Pareto set remains the same whether the status quo is reasonable or perfectly disgusting.

Those who advocate judging outcomes in terms of Pareto optimality need not value all Pareto optimal outcomes equally. Just as some advocate Pareto improvements from the status quo, others may want to include other restrictions on the Pareto set, such as demanding political outcomes that maximize the sum of individual utility or produce some equitable distribution. Our simulations loosely suggest that majority rule may be more capable of producing such outcomes than unanimity rule because it tends to produce outcomes in the center of the Pareto set. This is true even if the majority rule core is empty. Nevertheless, additional research is required before we can accurately draw such conclusions.

Few, if any, countries have adopted a constitution using unanimity rule.[3]. If scholars believe that constitutions should be both Pareto improvements from the status quo and Pareto optimal, then they may believe that history is full of missed opportunities. The use of less-inclusive voting rules for constitutional decision making may have allowed redistribution and produced outcomes that are not Pareto improvements. Now that history has created a long path of changes that may or may not be Pareto improvements, the world may have drifted to different outcomes that would have been avoided if unanimity rule was applied throughout time. On the one hand, any application of unanimity rule at this juncture might restrict societies

---

[3] To the best of our knowledge only a few countries have used it for day-to-day decision making. Some of these include the Polish Diet in the sixteenth to eighteenth centuries (Colomer, 2001), the Council of the European Union for some issue areas, the U.N. Security Council for nonprocedural decisions among its permanent members, and the U.S. Senate for unanimous consent agreements.

to less-desirable outcomes than if they consistently applied unanimity throughout history. On the other hand, if scholars are solely concerned about Pareto optimality, then they might be satisfied with the less-inclusive rules that have been widely used. These constitutions might actually be Pareto optimal.

In recognizing these limitations, we do not want to advocate one criterion over another. We simply want to advance the debate about which principles are best for constitutional design and to develop the side of the debate that has received less attention. Our role is that of analysts who want to show the implications of various assumptions and how these relationships might help us understand constitutional design. The most appropriate properties are left to the reader.

7.3 Broader Implications

When everything is said and done, we are faced with two questions that are at the very core of constitutional design: (1) Do constitutions really matter? (2) Can individuals really make themselves better off by agreeing to a specific set of rules?

In answering these questions, we have to do more than put our finger on some empirical evidence that suggests the answer is yes. We also have to determine whether these outcomes are normatively desirable. Despite David Hume's contention that positive statements, about what is, and normative statements, about what ought to be, are separate, one side can inform the other. Empirical conditions, such as individual valuations of different costs, can affect which k-majority rule a society ought to choose. If a society chooses institutions that are normatively desirable, then it may gain greater stability and increased public welfare. Hence, what may be normatively sound can be empirically sound as well.

The study of constitutional design has come a long way since *The Calculus of Consent*. Over the last two decades, the positive branch, which focuses on what is, has made remarkable progress thanks to the availability of data. This has made it possible to evaluate various empirical claims about parliamentary versus presidential systems, bicameralism versus unicameralism, and the implications of different voting rules.

One of the major findings is that successful institutional design is endogenous (Voigt, 2011). Put differently, effective constitutions depend on individuals and the context in which they live. And the context in which they live affects the constitutional design that they chose. Perhaps such empirical findings stem from endogeneity on the normative side. Institutions affect what is normatively desirable and normative values affect what institutions are adopted. Each society has to determine its own priorities, its own values, and create institutions that meet its needs. Copying a successful set of institutions from another country, like the United States, may make the task of constitutional design considerably easier, but it may not help a society address its own needs or create a constitution that individuals will obey.

With strong external involvement in the creation of constitutions in Iraq and Afghanistan, this lesson seems pertinent. Under different circumstances these countries may have adopted very different constitutions. Such constitutions may have seemed less desirable to the western eye, but they also may have avoided some of the recent constitutional crises within these countries and provided greater stability for the Middle East. Hence, allowing a society to create its own constitution based on its own values seems important. Hopefully, our small contribution can renew the debate and guide academics to help countries reach their goals.

References

Aldrich JH (1995) *Why Parties? The Origin and Transformation of Political Parties in America.* Chicago: University of Chicago Press.

Arrow K (1951) *Social Choice and Individual Values.* New York: John Wiley and Sons.

Austen-Smith D, Banks J (2005) *Positive Political Theory II: Strategy and Structure.* Ann Arbor: The University of Michigan Press.

Bailyn B (1993) *The Debate on the Constitution.* New York: Library of America.

Becker GS (1962) Irrational behavior and economic theory. *Journal of Political Economy* 70(1):1–13.

Berggren N (1996) Social order through constitutional choice. *Public Choice* 89:339–61.

Bianco WT, Lynch MS, Miller GJ, Sened I (2008) The constrained instability of majority rule: Experiments on the robustness of the uncovered set. *Political Analysis* 16:115–137.

Black D (1948) On the rationale of group decision-making. *The Journal of Political Economy* 56(1):23–34.

Brennan G, Hamlin A (2000) *Democratic Devices and Desires.* New York: Cambridge University Press.

Buchanan J (1962) The relevance of pareto optimality. *Journal of Conflict Resolution* 6(4):341–54.

Buchanan JM (1967) *Public Finance in Democratic Process.* Chapel Hill: The University of North Carolina Press.

Buchanan JM, Tullock G (1962) *The Calculus of Consent: Logical Foundations of Constitutional Democracy.* Ann Arbor: The University of Michigan Press.

Caplin A, Nalebuff B (1988) On 64%-majority rule. *Econometrica* 56(4):787–814.

Chamberlin JR, Cohen MD (1978) Toward applicable social choice theory: A comparison of social choice functions under spatial model assumptions. *American Political Science Review* 72(4):1341–56.

Clinton J, Jackman S, Rivers D (2004) The statistical analysis of roll call data. *American Political Science Review* 98(02):355–70.

Clinton JD, Meirowitz A (2004) Testing explanations of strategic voting in legislatures: A reexamination of the compromise of 1790. *American Journal of Political Science* 48(4):675–89.

Colomer JM (2001) *Political Institutions: Democracy and Social Choice.* New York: Oxford University Press.

Compte O, Jehiel P (2004) Bargaining over randomly generated offers: A new perspective on multi-party bargaining, c.E.R.A.S.-E.N.P.C., C.N.R.S., France.

Cornes R, Sandler T (1996) *The Theory of Externalities, Public Goods, and Club Goods,* 2nd ed. New York: Cambridge University Press.

Coughlin PJ (1992) *Probabilistic Voting Theory.* New York: Cambridge University Press.

Cox GW (1987) Electoral equilibrium under alternative voting institutions. *American Journal of Political Science* 31(1):82–108.

Crain WM, Tollison RD (1977) Legislative size and voting rules. *Journal of Legal Studies* 6(1):235–40.

Denzau A, Riker W, Shepsle K (1985) Farquharson and fenno: Sophisticated voting and home style. *American Political Science Review* 79(4):1117–34.

Diermeier D, Myerson RB (1999) Bicameralism and its consequences for the internal organization of legislatures. *American Economic Review* 89(5):1182–96.

Dietrich F, List C (2007) Arrows theorem in judgment aggregation. *Social Choice and Welfare* 29(1):19–33.

Dougherty KL, Edward J (2004) The pareto efficiency and expected costs of k-majority rules. *Politics Philosophy and Economics* 3(2):161–89.

Dougherty KL, Edward J (2005) A nonequilibrium analysis of unanimity rule, majority rule, and pareto. *Economic Inquiry* 43(4):855–64.

Dougherty KL, Edward J (2009) Odd or even: Assembly size and majority rule. *Journal of Politics* 71(02):733–47.

Dougherty KL, Edward J (2010a) The properties of simple vs. absolute majority rule: Cases where absences and abstentions are important. *Journal of Theoretical Politics* 22(1):85–122.

Dougherty KL, Edward J (2010b) Voting for a Pareto optimality: a multidimensional analysis. *Public Choice*, (forthcoming).

Dougherty KL, Heckelman J (2006) A pivotal voter from a pivotal state: Roger Sherman at the Constitutional Convention. *American Political Science Review* 100(2):297–302.

Dougherty KL, Pitts B, Moeller J, Ragan R (2010) An experimental study of the efficiency of unanimity rule and majority rule. *Public Choice*, (forthcoming).

Downs A (1957) *An Economic Theory of Democracy*. New York: Harper.

Duggan J (2006) Endogenous voting agendas. *Social Choice and Welfare* 27:495–530.

Enelow JM, Hinich MJ (1990) *Advances in the Spatial Theory of Voting*. New York: Cambridge University Press.

Farrand M (ed) (1966) *The Records of the Federal Convention of 1787*. New Haven: Yale University Press., 4 vols.

Farrell DM (2001) *Electoral Systems: A Comparative Introduction*. New York: Palgrave.

Feld SL, Grofman B, Miller N (1988) Centripetal forces in spatial voting: On the size of the yolk. *Public Choice* 59(1):37–50.

Felsenthal DS, Maoz Z, Rapoport A (1993) An empirical evaluation of six voting procedures: Do they really make any difference? *British Journal of Political Science* 23(01):1–27.

Fiorina MP, Plott CR (1978) Committee decisions under majority rule: An experimental study. *American Political Science Review* 72(2):575–98.

Fishburn PC (1973) *The Theory of Social Choice*. Princeton: Princeton University Press.

Fishburn PC (1987) *Interprofile Conditions and Impossibility*. London: Routledge.

Freixas J, Zwicker WS (2009) Anonymous yes–no voting with abstention and multiple levels of approval. *Games and Economic Behavior* 67(2):428–44.

Friedrich CJ (1963) *Man and His Government: An Empirical Theory of Politics.* New York: McGraw-Hill.

Gehrlein WV (2002a) Condorcet's paradox and the likelihood of its occurrence: Different perspectives on balanced preferences. *Theory and Decision* 52:171–99.

Gehrlein WV (2002b) Obtaining representations for probabilities of voting outcomes with effectively unlimited precision integer arithmetic. *Social Choice and Welfare* 19(3):503–12.

Gehrlein WV, Lepelley D (2010) *Voting Paradoxes and Group Coherence: The Condorcet Efficiency of Voting Rules.* New York: Springer Publishing.

Gode DK, Sunder S (1993) Allocative efficiency of markets with zero-intelligence traders: Market as a partial substitute for individual rationality. *Journal of Political Economy* 101(1):119–37.

Goldwin RA, Kaufman A (1988) *Constitution Makers on Constitution Making: The Experience of Eight Nations.* Washington, DC: American Enterprise Institute for Public Policy Research.

Grafstein R (1990) Missing the Archimedean point: Liberalism's institutional presuppositions. *American Political Science Review* 84(1):177–93.

Greif A, Laitin DD (2004) A theory of endogenous institutional change. *American Political Science Review* 98(4):633–52.

Groseclose T, Milyo J (2010) Sincere versus sophisticated voting in Congress: Theory and evidence. *Journal of Politics* 71(1):60–73.

Guttman JM (1998) Unanimity and majority rule: The calculus of consent reconsidered. *European Journal of Political Economy* 14(2):189–207.

Hammond TH, Miller GJ (1987) The core of the constitution. *American Political Science Review* 81(4):1155–74.

Hardin R (1988) Constitutional political economy: Agreement on rules. *British Journal of Political Science* 18(04):513–30.

Hardin R (1999) *Liberalism, Constitutionalism, and Democracy.* New York: Oxford University Press.

Head JG (1974) *Public Goods and Public Welfare.* Durham, NC: Duke University Press.

Heckelman JC (2003) Probabilistic Borda rule voting. *Social Choice and Welfare* 21(3):455–68.

Heckelman JC, Dougherty KL (2010a) Majority rule versus supermajority rules: Their effects on narrow and broad taxes. *Public Finance Review* 38(6):738–61.

Heckelman JC, Dougherty KL (2010b) What influenced delegate voting at the constitutional convention, mimeo, University of Georgia, Athens, GA.

Hinich M, Munger MC (1997) *Analytical Politics.* New York: Cambridge University Press.

Hobbes T ([1651] 1962) *Leviathan.* New York: Collier Macmillan.

Intriligator MD (1973) A probabilistic model of social choice. *Review of Economic Studies* 40(4):553–60.

Janis IL (1972) *Groupthink: psychological studies of policy decisions and fiascoes.* Boston: Houghton Mifflin.

Jillson C (1978) Voting bloc analysis in the Constitutional Convention: Implications for an interpretation of the Connecticut compromise. *Western Political Quarterly* 31(4):535–47.

Jillson C (1988) *Constitution Making: Conflict and Consensus in the Federal Convention of 1787*. New York: Agathon Press.

Koford KJ (1982) Centralized vote-trading. *Public Choice* 39(2):245–68.

Krehbiel K (1998) *Pivotal Politics: A Theory of U.S. Lawmaking*. Chicago: University of Chicago Press.

Laffont JJ (2000) *Incentives and Political Economy*. Oxford: Oxford University Press.

Laruelle A, Valenciano F (2010) Majorities with a quorum. *Journal of Theoretical Politics*, (forthcoming).

Lepelley D (1993) On the probability of electing the Condorcet loser. *Mathematical Social Sciences* 25(2):105–16.

Lepelley D, Pierron P, Valognes F (2000) Scoring rules, Condorcet efficiency, and social homogeneity. *Theory and Decision* 49(2):175–96.

Lijphart A (1999) *Patterns of Democracy: Government Forms and Performance in Thirty-Six Countries*. New Haven: Yale University Press.

Lindahl E ([1919] 1967) *Classics in the Theory of Public Finance*, New York: St. Martin's Press., chap Just Taxation – a Positive Solution, pp 168–76.

Lipset SM (1963) *The First New Nation: The United States in Historical and Comparative Perspective*. New York: Basic Books.

Locke J ([1690] 1988) *Two Treatises of Government*. New York: Cambridge University Press.

Lord C (1984) Roll calls of the Continental Congresses and the congresses of the confederation, 1777–1789. ICPSR data set 7537.

Lutz DS (2006) *Principles of Constitutional Design*. New York: Cambridge University Press.

May KO (1952) A set of independent necessary and sufficient conditions for simple majority decision. *Econometrica* 20:680–84.

McCarty N, Poole KT, Rosenthal H (2005) *Polarized America: The Dance of Ideology and Unequal Riches*. Cambridge, MA: MIT Press.

McGann AJ (2006) *The Logic of Democracy: Reconciling Equality, Deliberation, and Minority Protection*. Ann Arbor: University of Michigan Press.

McGuire RA (2003) *To Form a More Perfect Union: A New Economic Interpretation of the United States Constitution*. Oxford: Oxford University Press.

McKelvey RD (1976) Intransitivities in mulitdimensional voting models and some implications for agenda control. *Journal of Economic Theory* 12:472–82.

McKelvey RD (1986) Covering, dominance, and institution-free properties of social choice. *American Journal of Political Science* 30(2):283–314.

McKelvey RD, Ordeshook PC (1984) An experimental study of the effects of procedural rules on committee behavior. *Journal of Politics* 46(1):182–205.

Merrill S (1984) A comparison of efficiency of multicandidate electoral systems. *American Journal of Political Science* 28(1):23–48.

Miller GJ, Hammond TH (1990) Committees and the core of the constitution. *Public Choice* 66(3):201–27.

Mueller D (1996) *Constitutional Democracy*. New York: Oxford University Press.

Mueller D (2001) The importance of uncertainty in a two-stage theory of constitutions. *Public Choice* 108(3):223–58.

Mueller D (2003) *Public Choice III*. New York: Cambridge University Press.

Niemi RG, Weisberg HF (1968) A mathematical solution for the probability of the paradox of voting. *Behavioral Science* 13:317–23.

Niou EM, Ordeshook PC (1985) Universalism in Congress. *American Journal of Political Science* 29(2):246–58.

North DC, Weingast BR (1989) Constitutions and commitment: The evolution of institutional governing public choice in seventeenth-century England. *Journal of Economic History* 49(4):803–32.

Nozick R (1974) *Anarchy, State, and Utopia*. New York: Basic Books.

Nurmi H (1987) *Comparing Voting Systems*. New York: Springer.

Nurmi H (1992) An assessment of voting system simulations. *Public Choice* 73(4):459–87.

Nurmi H, Uusi-Heikkila Y (1986) Computer simulations of approval and plurality voting: The frequency of weak Pareto violations and Condorcet loser choices in impartial cultures. *European Journal of Political Economy* 2(1):47–59.

Olson M (1965) *The Logic of Collective Action: Public Goods and the Theory of Groups*. Cambridge, MA: Harvard University Press.

Ordeshook P (1986) *Game Theory and Political Theory*. New York: Cambridge University Press.

Ostrom E (1990) *Governing the Commons*. New York: Cambridge University Press.

Palfrey TR (1984) Spatial equilibrium with entry. *Review of Economic Studies* 51(1):139–56.

Penn EM (2009) A model of farsighted voting. *American Journal of Political Science* 53(1):36–54.

Peress M (2009) Estimating proposal and status quo locations using voting and cosponsorship data, mimeo, University of Rochester, Rochester, NY.

Plott CR (1967) A notion of equilibrium and its possibility under majority rule. *American Economic Review* 57:787–806.

Poole K, Rosenthal H (1984) The polarization of American politics. *Journal of Politics* 46(4):1061–79.

Poole KT, Rosenthal H (1997) *Congress: A Poltical-Economic History of Roll Call Voting*. New York: Oxford University Press.

Pope J, Treier S (2009) Mapping dimensions of the conflict at the federal convention of 1787, mimeo, University of Minnesota, Twin Cities, MN.

Przeworski A (2005) Democracy as an equilibrium. *Public Choice* 123(3):253–73.

Rae DW (1969) Decision rules and individual values in constitutional choice. *American Political Science Review* 63(1):40–56.

Rae DW (1975) The limits of consensual decision. *American Political Science Review* 69(4):1270–94.

Rasch B (1995) *Parliamentary Voting Procedures*, New York: St. Martin's Press, pp 488–527.

Rasch BE (2000) Parliamentary floor voting procedures and agenda setting in Europe. *Legislative Studies Quarterly* 25(1):3–23.

Regenwetter M, Groffman B, Marley A, Tsetlin I (2006) *Behavioral Social Choice: Probabilistic Models, Statistical Inference, and Applications.* New York: Cambridge University Press.

Reilly B (2002) Social choice in the South Seas: Electoral innovation and the Borda count in the Pacific Island countries. *International Political Science Review* 23(4):355–72.

Riker WH (1962) Review of the calculus of consent by James M. Buchanan and Gordon Tullock. *Midwest Journal of Political Science* 6(4):408–11.

Riker WH (1980) Implications from the disequilibrium of majority rule for the study of institutions. *American Political Science Review* 74(2):432–46.

Riker WH (1982) *Liberalism against populism.* Prospect Heights, IL: Waveland Press.

Riker WH (1992) The justification of bicameralism. *International Political Science Review* 13(1):101–16.

Riker WH, Brams SJ (1973) The paradox of vote trading. *American Political Science Review* 67(4):1235–47.

Riker WH, Calvert RL, Mueller JE, Wilson RK (1996) *The Strategy of Rhetoric: Campaigning for the American Constitution.* New Haven: Yale University Press.

Roberts KW (1980) Possibility theorems with interpersonally comparable welfare levels. *Review of Economic Studies* 47(2):409–20.

Rogowski R (1974) *Rational Legitimacy: A Theory of Political Support.* Princeton: Princeton University Press.

Rousseau JJ ([1762] 1997) *The Social Contract and Other Later Political Writings.* New York: Cambridge University Press.

Rowley CK (2004) *The Selected Works of Gordon Tullock.* Indianapolis, IN: Liberty Fund.

Saari DG (1995) *Basic Geometry of Voting.* New York: Springer-Verlag.

Saari DG (1999) Explaining all three-alternative voting outcomes. *Journal of Economic Theory* 87(2):313–55.

Saari DG (2003) Unsettling aspects of voting theory. *Economic Theory* 22(3):529–55.

Saari DG (2008) *Disposing Dictators, Demystifying Voting Paradoxes: Social Choice Analysis.* New York: Cambridge University Press.

Saari DG, Barney S (2003) Consequences of reversing preferences. *The Mathematical Intelligencer* 25(4):17–31.

Schofield NJ (1978) Instability of simple dynamic games. *Review of Economic Studies* 45:575–94.

Sen AK (1979a) *Collective Choice and Social Welfare.* New York: North-Holland.

Sen AK (1979b) Utilitarianism and welfarism. *Journal of Philosophy* 76(9):463–89.

Shepsle KA (1979) Institutional arrangements and equilibrium in multidimensional voting models. *American Journal of Political Science* 23(1):27–59.

Shleifer A, Treisman D (2001) *Without a Map: Political Tactics and Economic Reform in Russia.* Cambridge, MA: The MIT Press.

Spindler ZA (1990) Constitutional design for a rent-seeking society: Voting rule choice. *Constitutional Political Economy* 1(3):73–82.

Council of State Governments (2009) *The Book of the States.* Lexington, KY: The Council of State Governments.

Stewart C (2001) *Analyzing Congress.* New York: W.W. Norton.

Tsebelis G (1990) *Nested Games: Rational Choice in Comparative Politics.* Berkeley: University of California Press.

Tsebelis G (2002) *Veto Players: How Political Institutions Work.* New York: Russell Sage Foundation.

Tullock G (1998) *On Voting: A Public Choice Approach.* Northampton, MA: Edward Elgar.

Tversky A, Kahneman D (1974) Judgment under uncertainty: Heuristics and biases. *Science* 185(4157):1124–31.

Van Newenhizen J (1992) The Borda method is most likely to respect the Condorcet principle. *Economic Theory* 2(1):69–83.

Voigt S (1997) Positive constitutional economics: A survey. *Public Choice* 90(1):11–53.

Voigt S (2011) Positive constitutional economics II: a survey of recent developments. *Public Choice* 146(1–2):205–56.

Weimer DL, Vining AR (2005) *Policy Analysis: Concepts and Practice*, 4th ed. Saddle River, NJ: Prentice-Hall.

Wicksell K ([1896] 1967) *Classics in the Theory of Public Finance*, 3rd ed., New York: McGraw-Hill., chap New Principle of Just Taxation, pp 72–118.

Young HP (1974) An axiomitizatoin of Borda's rule. *Journal of Economic Theory* 9(2):43–52.

Index

LaVergne, TN USA
31 March 2011
222391LV00007B/88/P